# Gospel Hope for Anxious Hearts

–

Trading Fear and Worry for
the Peace of God

Charles Haddon Spurgeon

Gospel Hope for Anxious Hearts

© 2017 by Cross-Points Books

All Scripture is taken from the *King James Version.*

Material sourced from The Metropolitan Tabernacle Pulpit Sermons

ISBN-13: 978-1539690818

ISBN-10: 1539690814

# CONTENTS

# SERIES INTRODUCTION

The Rich Theology Made Accessible Series seeks to bolster the faith of busy Christians by making rich theology from time past more accessible.

Current Titles:
- Volume 1: *The Chief Exercise of Faith: John Calvin on Prayer*
- Volume 2: *Gospel Hope for Anxious Hearts: Trading Fear and Worry for the Peace of God* by Charles Spurgeon

Visit Cross-Points.org/richtheology to learn more or to explore additional titles.

# FOREWORD

Like a picture, a good Internet meme is worth 1,000 words.

One meme I love (but probably shouldn't) is the one where a dog in a hat is seated on a chair in a burning house with a goofy smile. His speech bubble says, "*This is fine.*"[1]

The meme comes from a larger comic that shows the spread of the fire in the house, to which the dog says, "I'm okay with the events that are currently unfolding"—trying to talk himself out of the great danger he is in. After another sip of coffee, the flames reach the dog's arm and it begins to melt.

*"That's okay, things are going to be okay."*

The last square shows the dog melting in the fire that overtook the room he was sitting in.

Things didn't end fine.

For many, this is a modern day parable of the anxiety in our lives. We are bombarded by stress in every area of life: family, finances, work, and church. Instead of running from the burning house to safety and peace, we tell ourselves, "This is fine."

Anxiety is a lot like a fire. A difficult situation at work, a negative comment from your spouse, or thoughts about your child's future can stoke the fires of anxiety. The more anxious thoughts you have, the more the fire grows until it blows up in an outburst of anger or a full-blown panic attack. The fire spreads from where it starts and, unbeknownst to us, overtakes other areas of our lives.

Some scientists suggest that 18% of us in the United States suffer from an anxiety disorder.[2] They also argue that North America, with the US carrying its fair share or responsibility, is the most anxious place in the world today.[3] Clearly we have a problem. I'm no historian, let alone psychologist, but I would argue that we are the most stressed people in history. It appears our relative prosperity, advancements in technology, and countless life options has only caused more anxiety as we figure out how to raise our families, spend our money, and keep up with the Joneses' perfect life. (And if only the Joneses didn't constantly remind you of their perfect life on Instagram!)

Anxiety is an equal opportunity offender: it can strike rich or poor, male or female, believer or unbeliever, American or Indian or American Indian. Left unchecked, it can bring serious consequences (even if it doesn't melt our faces off like the dog's in the meme example):

- Physical effects of anxiety include headaches, heart palpitations, increased blood pressure, panic attacks, and an inability to relax or sleep. More serious physical effects of long-term anxiety include heart attacks, cancer, or diabetes.[4]

- Psychological effects of anxiety might drain attention span, the ability to retain information, hinder work performance and communication skills, or lead to depression.[5]
- Spiritual effects include a lack of joy and peace (see Matthew 6:25-34; Philippians 4:6-7), damaged relationships with God and others, and even choking out potential for saving faith (Luke 8:14).

The worst part is, we can get so used to stress that we don't even notice it. Or if we do notice it, we give up trying to change. This is tragic because it misses the "peace that passes all understanding" that is always ours for the taking in Christ (Philippians 4:6-7). Our view of God shrinks as our anxieties grow.

I have believed worry is a sin for a long time.[6] Sometimes when I notice I am worrying, I worry more, getting sucked into a never-ending downward spiral of anxiety.

What we need to do in such situations is focus on Jesus and not our anxiety. (Easier said than done!) As sinful people, we will always have sin to discourage us. Focusing on our sin is like trying to clean mud off of ourselves with a muddy cloth—all we will do will be spread around the filth and get frustrated! When we look to Jesus for help and cleanness, He hoses us down, dries us off, and comforts us in our situation. This is the continual hope we have in the gospel.

## Precious Truths Forged in the Furnace of Affliction

Charles Spurgeon (1834–1892) was no stranger to anxiety; he struggled with several health issues off and on his entire adult life. His wife was often sick as well. His ministry faced sharp criticism most of his life and survivor's guilt plagued him after seven people were trampled to death in an auditorium in which he was scheduled to preach.[7]

Spending so much time in the furnace of affliction taught Spurgeon the gospel's hope for trying times. He knew the peace of God in Christ could overcome the toughest and direst of situations. These struggles colored Spurgeon's ministry and caused him to comfort thousands with the healing balm of the gospel through his preaching. He knew that only with a rock-solid faith in Christ's love and acceptance can we truly say, "This is fine."

In ***Gospel Hope for Anxious Hearts: Trading Fear and Worry for the Peace of God***, readers will find ten sermons by Spurgeon on anxiety, fear, and rest. My hope and prayer is that as you read, your soul will be lifted to see the beauty and sufficiency of our Risen Savior and the glorious, yet immensely practical hope he offers us today.

*"The man who is full of care, is ripe for any sin, but he who has cast his care on God stands securely, neither shall the evil one be able to touch him!" — Charles Spurgeon*

Kevin Halloran
Writer at Anchored in Christ (www.kevinhalloran.net)
Pastoral Trainer at Leadership Resources International
(www.leadershipresources.org)
Schaumburg, IL
September 2017

[1] Now internet-famous, this originated in the web comic Gunshow. (See "This is Fine" on KnowYourMeme.com.)
[2] See "A systematic review of reviews on the prevalence of anxiety disorders in adult populations" on Wiley Online Library. Accessed September 28, 2016 from http://onlinelibrary.wiley.com/doi/10.1002/brb3.497/.
[3] Ibid.
[4, 5] Gary Collins shares this and more in *Christian Counseling: A Comprehensive Guide Third Edition* (2007), pages 141-149.
[6] This isn't to say there may be a place for biological treatment to stress. But trust me, I'm not the guy you want to hear talk about that.
[7] For more on Spurgeon's sorrows, read *Spurgeon's Sorrows* by Zach Eswine. For more on controversy in Spurgeon's life, read *The Forgotten Spurgeon* by Iain Murray.

# 1
# A CURE FOR CARE

*"Casting all your care upon him; for he careth for you."*
*—1 Peter 5:7*

*"The man who is full of care, is ripe for any sin,*
*but he who has cast his care on God stands securely,*
*neither shall the evil one be able to touch him!"*

~

No one precept contains the whole of a believer's duty; but usually in Scripture, the precepts rise one above the other, like those stone steps by which the traveller in Egypt ascends to the pinnacle of the pyramid. Ye must first plant your feet firmly upon the preceding duty, before ye shall be able fully to climb to the next command. Let me, then, call your attention to the precept which precedes my text: "Humble yourselves therefore under the mighty hand of God, that he may exalt you in due time." You know, beloved, that there are some selfish, carnal cares which we must not cast upon God; it were an insult to him; it were an act of infamy on our part if we should venture to ask for his assistance in them. Those are cares which would never molest us at all if we were obedient to the precept: "Humble yourselves therefore under the

1

mighty hand of God." This cuts off the head at once of many of those anxieties into which Christians sometimes fall. For instance, covetous cares—if I desire to get and grasp more than is absolutely necessary, that I may hastily grow rich, I cannot on my knees ask God to carry this care for me, because it is none of his sending. He has taught me to say, "Give us this day our daily bread," and he has given me a blessed example in Agur, that I may pray, "Give me neither poverty nor riches;" but I cannot go on my knees before God, honestly, as a miser, and ask that he would enable me to add house to house, and field to field. But then, that care I never ought to indulge, and I never should endure it if I attended to the precept, "Humble yourselves therefore under the mighty hand of God." There is, also, the care of ambition, when men desire to attain honours, eminence, and fame; to stand foremost, to be exalted upon the pinnacle, to be looked up to by all, and to be almost adored by some. But if we allow ambition to creep into our minds, we cannot go to God with it. It is a care which we dare not cast on God, for that were to empty the filth of our house upon the altar of God's sanctuary. But then, I say, it is a care which would never fret us, if our souls were lowly before the Lord.

There are those cares too, which we make for ourselves—those anxieties which anticipate the future— those foolish fears which are only created in our brain, and which vex the head, and then fret the heart—we cannot ask God to take those upon himself; cares which have no existence except in our own fancies, we can scarcely cast on God. But then, beloved, we should never have them if we "humbled ourselves under the mighty hand of God." Then, in such a state of subjection to the divine will, and of resignation to the eternal purpose, our soul would sit in quiet and be still, and our spirit would not agitate itself with frivolities which it has itself imagined, with fancies which have no origin but in its own imagination. Oh that ye may have grace to obey the preceding command, and then I think, without any limitation, I may address you in the words of the text: "Casting all your care upon him; for he careth for you." I repeat, sinful cares we cannot cast on God; but then, obeying the precept, "Humble yourselves," would uproot such vexations. He that is down, need fear no fall. He whose soul is even as a weaned child will fret and cry no more.

In addressing you this morning from so rich a text as this, I would rather pray that the Holy Spirit may deliver you from carefulness, than attempt to deliver you from it myself, for I am not even able to obey this precept myself, much less shall I enable you to do it. Only when the Spirit of God is upon the preacher can *he* cast his cares upon his God, and he is convinced by experience, that only as the Holy Ghost shall enable you, will *you* be able to do the same. However, that our word may be the means of your comfort and of your strengthening, let us speak on this wise. First, for a few minutes, *let us expound this disease of care*, giving some description of it; secondly, *let us manifest the blessed remedy of the text*, endeavouring in God's name, to apply it; and lastly, *let us hold out the sweet inducement of the second part of the sentence*, in order that believers may be led to attempt the practising of the precept, "He careth for you."

## I. First, then, let us endeavour to describe the disease of care.

The care mentioned in the text, even though it be exercised upon legitimate objects, (and in this it differs from the cares of which I spoke just now, which were cares concerning wrong objects;) care even when exercised upon legitimate objects if carried to excess, hath in itself *the nature of sin*. This will be clear if you think for a moment that anything which is a transgression of God's command is sin, and if there were no other command, the one in our text being broken would involve us in iniquity. But it is a precept earnestly repeated by our Saviour many times, it is one which the apostles have reiterated again and again, and one which cannot be neglected without involving transgression. Besides, the very essence of anxious care is the imagining that we are wiser than God, and the thrusting of ourselves into his place, to do for him that which we dream he either cannot or will not do; we attempt to think of that which we fancy he will forget; or we labour to take upon ourselves that burden which he either is not able or willing to carry for us. Now, this impertinence, this presumption, what if I say, this audacity, has in it the very nature of sin, to attempt to know better than God, to snatch from his hand the helm by which he guides affairs, to attempt to correct his charts, to remap his providence, this indeed is such an impertinence that as the guardian Scripture pushes back the intruder, it demands of him, "Art thou also one of the King's counsel? What doest thou here? He took no counsel with thee when he made the heavens and the earth and balanced the clouds, and stretched out the skies like a tent to dwell in, how darest thou come hither and offer advice to perfect wisdom, and aid to omnipotent strength?" There is in anxious care the very nature of sin.

But, further, these anxious cares very frequently lead to other sins, sometimes to *overt acts o, transgression.* The tradesman who is not able to leave his business with God, may be tempted to indulge in the tricks of trade; nay, he may not only be tempted, but he may be prevailed upon to put out an unholy hand with which to help himself. The professional or literary man, if he has no firm trust in providence, may lend his skill to indirect and unlawful ends; and each man if he have no other snare, will be tried with this—to forsake prayer and to forget the promise in order to trust to the wisdom of a friend, or to the natural sagacity of some mentor in whom he puts confidence. Now, this is forsaking the fountain to go to the broken cisterns, a crime which was laid against Israel of old, a wrath provoking iniquity. Even if it led to no other act save this sin of preferring the counsel of man to the direction of God, excessive anxiety were to be reprobated and detested. But think, my brethren, of the many sins which our anxieties engender in our hearts. Our unbelief which makes us doubt our God, our want of love which is proven by our distrust of love, our want of hope which puts out our eyes so that we cannot see the clear shining after the rain. Think, my brethren, how we fret and mistrust and thus vex the Spirit of God, and often cause him to depart from us, so that our prayers are hindered, so that our example is marred, so that we give ourselves rather to self-seeking than to seeking God. All these things are sins, the grapes of Gomorrha which grow on the vines of our cares. These base-born cares are the plentiful mothers of transgressions. Distrust is the egg out of which many a mischief is hatched; we indulge in these cares and think surely we are doing no wrong, whereas the indulgence in them is in itself a crime, and is besides a tempter which guides us onward to the commission of other iniquities, for the man that is full of care is ripe for any sin, but he who has cast his care on God standeth securely, neither shall the evil one be able to touch him.

To proceed further in uncovering this disease. As it is in itself sin, and the mother of sin, we note again that *it brings misery*, for where sin is, sorrow shall soon follow. He who would have his spirit bowed down even to the very earth, has only to fix his thoughts upon himself and his circumstances, instead of looking to God and his promises. Some of you are placed in a very happy position in life, but my dear brethren, you can make yourselves miserable if you please. Others of you are put in what the world considers unhappy circumstances, but if God enable you, you can be supremely blessed. Poverty does not necessarily involve sorrow, nor do riches of themselves bring peace or happiness. If any of you wish for misery you need not go out of your own house, there is no need to travel far for causes of discontent; you can be surfeited with plenty and be poor; you can dwell in the midst of peace and be disturbed; you can possess the richest prosperity and yet be afflicted. We, to a very great extent make our own position. God ordains providence, and either grace makes us happy, or sin racks us with pain. God does not make our misery; the cause of our trouble lies at our own door, not at his. Do you see that Christian there with the sparkling eye, and the light footstep, the man who is swift to run upon his Master's errands? that man has many troubles, but when he wakes in the morning if he retains remembrance of them, he bows his knee and leaves them with his God: he goes home, and the day has had much of sorrow in it, but he shakes the weight from his own shoulder and leaves his burden upon God. That man, with all his troubles, is more blessed than yonder professor, who has very little to vex him except that he vexes himself, by making every little thing a ground for fretfulness, magnifying every small mischance into a strange calamity, and by losing all patience, when all things suit not his proud will and dainty taste. Oh brethren! it is an ill thing for Christians to be sad. Let them rejoice, "Rejoice in the Lord always," but they never can so long as they indulge in anxious cares.

Besides this, these anxious cares do not only lead us into sin, and destroy our peace of mind, but they also *weaken us for usefulness*. When one has left all his cares at home, how well he can work for his Master, but when those cares tease us in the pulpit, it is hard preaching the gospel. When cares buzz in the ear, the music of grace is hard to hear. What would you say of your workman who should come to you in the morning with a heavy piece of family furniture upon his back. He calls himself your porter, he is about to carry your goods, and you see him going out of the door with your load, which is properly proportioned to his strength, but beside that he is carrying a heavy piece of his own upon his shoulders. You say to him, "My good man, what are you doing there?" "Oh sir, I am only loaded with household stuff." I think you would say, "Well, but you are not fit to do my work which you are engaged to do. I do not employ you to carry your own load, I had you here to carry mine." "But sir," says he, "I am so weak, I cannot carry both." "Then leave yours alone," say you, "and carry mine." Or to use another simile. There was a great king who once employed a merchant in his service as an ambassador to Foreign courts. Now the merchant before he went away, said to the king, "My own business requires all my care, and though I am always willing to be your majesty's servant, yet if I attend to your business as I ought, I am sure my own will be ruined." "Well," said the king, "you take care of my business, and I will take care of yours. Use your best endeavours, and I will answer for it that you shall be nothing the loser for the zeal which you take from yourself to give to me." And so our God says to us, as his servants, "Do my work, and I will do yours. Serve me and I will serve you." Like Peter,—Peter is fishing, Christ needs a pulpit to preach in. He borrows Peter's boat, and preaches in it; well what about Peter's fishing? Oh the Master will take care of that, for no sooner is the sermon done than he says, "Launch into the deep, and let down your nets for a draught," and Peter gets more in ten minutes through having lent his boat to his Master, than he might have done in ten weeks, if he had been fishing on his own account. Leave your cares with God, and care for him,

"Make you *his* service your delight,
*Your* wants shall be *his* care."

The subject would not be complete if I did not add that these carking cares, of whose guilt perhaps we think so little, *do very great damage to our blessed and holy cause.* Your sad and miserable countenances hinder souls who are anxious, and they present a ready excuse for souls who are careless. "Look," say they, "look, that man is a Christian man, the whole of the winters of a century have left their stormrifts on his forehead, and all the winds of ages seem to have ruffled his brow, he has no peace, no joy;—Who would be a Christian to be so miserable?" Thus the careless man says he will not have hell here, he will leave that for hereafter, while even anxious spirits say, "It cannot be that this religion is true, for if it were really true one would think it would be able to support its followers in the troubles of life. If God's Word be true that God will sustain his people, then Christians would be sustained, and believers would be cheered and comforted; but I see that they are as much fretful as other men, as impatient as they are, and that So-and-so, who makes a profession, is quite as weak, quite as easily bowed before the storm as yonder man who has no God in whom to trust, and no promises on which to lean." Ah! let it not be said so Christian through you; open not the enemy's mouth to blaspheme; let not the dragon find food through you who are of the seed of the woman, but rather seek, casting your care on God, to disentangle yourself of all personal hindrances that you may be avenged upon your Master's adversaries as a good soldier of Jesus Christ. I close the description of this matter by saying that in the most frightful manner cares have brought many to the poisoned cup, the halter, and the knife, and hundreds to the madhouse. What makes the constant increase of our lunatic asylums; why is it that in almost every country in England new asylums have to be erected, wing after wing being added to these buildings in which the imbecile and the raving are confined? It is because we *will* carry what we have no business to carry— our own cares, and until there shall be a general keeping of the day of rest throughout England, and until there shall be a more general resting of our souls and all we have upon God, we must expect to hear of increasing suicides and increasing lunacies. So long as the present system of competition in business shall continue—and there seems no hope that it will ever cease, for rather the signs of the times forbode that the battle will grow sterner every day— it will become a more stern duty with each of us to cast our care on God, unless we would see reason reel, and would be howling maniacs in our cells. Oh, for your own sake and for your children's sake, for Christ's sake and for his Church's sake, I pray you spoil not the fair house which God has builded, cast not out the lovely tenant, leave not the temple of the Lord to be the prison-house of madness. Away with evil cares if you would still be a man.

## II. I shall now want your attention to the second part of the subject, the blessed remedy to be applied.

Somebody must carry these cares. If I cannot do it myself, can I find any one who will? My Father who is in heaven stands waiting to be my burden-bearer. With broad shoulders, with omnipotence as his strength, he says "My child, roll thy burden upon thy God." Blessed privilege, dare I neglect it; can I be wicked enough to reject it and to bear my cares myself. Here is the blessed remedy, "Cast thy burden upon the Lord and he will sustain thee."

Now in order rather to apply this remedy than to describe it, by the help of God's Holy Spirit I will mention some of those fears, those cares which are legitimate enough in their objects, but which can only be relieved by leaving them with God. One of the first and most natural cares with which we are vexed is *the care for daily bread.* "I should be content" says one "with food and raiment; if I can but provide things honest in the sight of all men, and see my family cared for, I shall then be happy." "But" saith one, "what shall I eat, what shall I drink, wherewithal shall I be clothed? without a situation, having therefore no opportunity to earn my livelihood; without substance, having therefore nothing to look upon by which I may be supported without labour; without friend or patron who might give me his generous assistance; what shall I do?" You are a Christian are you; you must use all diligence, that is your duty: but oh, if God shall help you, mingle no fretfulness with the diligence, no impatience with your suffering, and no distrust with your trials. No, remember what Jesus has said so sweetly to the point, "Behold the fowls of the air: for they sow not, neither do they reap, nor gather into barns; yet your Heavenly Father feedeth them. Are ye not much better than they? Which of you by taking thought can add one cubit unto his stature? And why take ye thought for raiment? Consider the lilies of the field, how they grow; they toil not, neither do they spin: and yet I say unto you That even Solomon in his glory was not arrayed like one of these. Wherefore, if God so clothe the grass of the field, which to-day is, and to-morrow is cast into the oven, shall he not much more clothe you, O ye of little faith? Therefore, take no thought, saying, What shall we eat? or, What shall we drink? or, Wherewithal shall we be clothed? (for after all these things do the Gentiles seek:) for your Heavenly Father knoweth that ye have need of all these things. But seek ye first the kingdom of God, and his righteousness; and all these things shall be added unto you." Such a care as that I say is natural enough, and to bid a man shake it off when he is in actual need is cruelly absurd, unless you have a sure consolation to offer him; but you can say, "Cast your trial upon God." Use your most earnest endeavours, humble yourself under the mighty hand of God; if you cannot do one thing do another; if you cannot earn your bread as a gentleman earn it as a poor man; if you cannot earn it by the sweat of your brains do it by the sweat of your brow, do something for an honest living; sweep a crossing if you cannot do anything else, for if a man will not work neither let him eat; but having brought yourself to that, if still every door is shut, "Trust in the Lord and do good, so shalt thou dwell in the land, and verily thou shalt be fed."

*Business men*, who have not exactly to hunt for the necessaries of life, are often tormented with the anxieties of large transactions and extended commerce. The failures of others, frequent bad debts, changes in the markets, monetary pressures, and sudden panics, cause a world of trouble. Through our fashion of credit in this age, it is very hard for a Christian to conduct business in the sober substantial fashion which a tender conscience would prefer. "Owe no man anything,"—if that could be interwoven into the system of trade, it would I do not doubt, cure ten thousand ills which now grow out of that credit system, which seems to be unavoidable, but which I am sure involves many of the crimes which are committed, and very much of the care which racks business men. Well, through the present high-pressure system of trade there is naturally much care. If any man here can say that he can go into his office having many in his employ, and never at all have care, I should think he must be a *rara avis* in the world, surely he might walk till he dropped with weariness before he would meet with another of the same order. But if there be a brother here who has a business so extensive that he does not sleep at night, that he lies there tossing on his bed, thinking about this servant who may have robbed him, or about that vessel that is out at sea, or about the low prices of a certain article which has gone down since he laid in a large stock, and all those little things which all of you know—then I say, "Brother, hold hard here, what are you doing? what are you doing? Are you sure that in this you have used your best prudence and wisdom, and your best industry, and given it your best attention?" "Yes." Well then, what more have you to do? Suppose you like to weep all night, will that keep your ship from going on the Goodwin sands? Suppose you could cry your eyes out, will that make a thief honest? Suppose you could fret yourself till you could not eat, would that raise the price of goods? One would think if you were just to say, "Well, I have done all that is to be done, now I will leave it with God," that you might go about your business and have the full use of your senses to attend to it. Whereas now, you fritter away your senses, and then commit blunders, and so multiply your troubles by that very fretfulness by which you hoped to remove them. There—let them alone! We say, "Leave well alone," but I say, "Leave ill alone," leave them both alone, and with your two hands, for you will want both hands to do it,—with the hand of prayer, "In everything by prayer and supplication, making known your wants unto God," and with the other hand, the hand of faith, trusting in God—lift your load right off from your own shoulders, and let the whole crushing weight be left with your eternal God, for "he will sustain thee, he will never suffer the righteous to be moved."

Another anxiety of a personal kind which is very natural, and indeed very proper if it be not carried to excess, is the care of your *children*. Blessed be God for our children. We do not sympathise with those who look upon them as afflictions, for we believe them still to be a heritage of the Lord. But what anxieties they involve, how shall we bring them up, how shall they be provided for? Will they honour their parents, or will they bring disgrace upon the name they bear? A child may be the greatest curse his parents ever had, while he may be their choicest comfort. "All these," as an old puritan said, "are doubtful blessings, and may be certain curses," yet I will not have it that there is any doubt about their being blessings, as God sends them. A Christian parent must have care about his children, and all the more because he is a Christian, since he will not be satisfied with their getting on in business, he will never be content till his children walk in the truth. Mother, father, you have prayed for your children, you trust you have set them a holy example, you labour day by day to teach them the truth as it is in Jesus; you have travailed in birth for their souls till Christ be formed in them; it is well, now let your souls quietly expect the blessing, leave your offspring with God; cast your sons and daughters upon their father's God; let no impatience intrude if they are not converted in your time, and let no distrust distract your mind if they should seem to belie your hopes. I met yesterday with a few verses, which sound like the warblings of an American songstress; they exactly suit my subject, and in reading them in private they have touched my heart. Excuse me therefore, if though I never read a sermon, I should for once read a part of one.

"The Master has come over Jordan,"
Said Hannah, the mother, one day;
"He is healing the people who throng Him,
With a touch of His finger, they say.
And now I shall carry the children,
Little Rachel, and Samuel, and John
I shall carry the baby, Esther,
For the Lord to look upon."
The father looked at her kindly,
But he shook his head, and smiled:
"Now, who but a doating mother
Would think of a thing so wild?
If the children were tortured by demons,
Or dying of fever 'twere well;
Or had they the taint of the leper,
Like many in Israel."
"Nay, do not hinder me, Nathan;
I feel such a burden of care:
If I carry it to the Master,
Perhaps I shall leave it there.
If He lay His hand on the children,
My heart will be lighter, I know:
For a blessing for ever and ever
Will follow them as they go."
So, over the hills of Judah,
Along by the vine-rows green,
With Esther asleep on her bosom,
And Rachel her brothers between;
'Mong the people who hung on His teaching,
Or waited His touch and His word,
Through the row of proud Pharisees listening,
She pressed to the feet of the Lord.
"Now, why should'st thou hinder the Master,"

Said Peter, "with children like these?
Seest not how, from morning till evening,
He teacheth and healeth disease?"
Then Christ said, "Forbid not the children,
Permit them to come unto Me!"
And He took in His arms little Esther,
And Rachel He set on His knee:
And the heavy heart of the mother
Was lifted all earth-care above,
As He laid His hands on the brothers,
And blest them with tenderest love;
As He said of the babes in His bosom,
"Of such are the kingdom of heaven;"
And strength for all duty and trial
That hour to her spirit was given.
Thus do ye, and thus inherit the blessing.

But each Christian will in his time have personal troubles of a higher order, namely, *spiritual cares*. He is begotten again unto a lively hope, but he fears that his faith will yet die. He hopes he has some spark of spiritual joy, but there are dark and dreary nights which lower over him, and he fears that his lamp will die out in darkness. As yet he has been victorious, but he trembles lest he should one day fall by the hand of the enemy. Beloved, I beseech thee; cast this care upon God for he careth for you. "I am persuaded that he that hath begun a good work in you will carry it on and perfect it unto the day of Christ." He hath said, "I will never leave thee, nor forsake thee." "The fountains shall depart, and the hills be removed; but my kindness shall not depart from thee, neither shall the covenant of my peace be removed, saith the Lord that hath mercy on thee." "When thou passest through the waters, I will be with thee; and through the rivers, they shall not overflow thee: when thou walkest through the fire, thou shalt not be burned; neither shall the flame kindle upon thee." "No good thing will I withhold from them that walk uprightly." "I give unto my sheep eternal life, and they shall never perish, neither shall any man pluck them out of my hand." Why, one might keep you all this morning, and this afternoon and evening too, repeating the precious promises of God, and we might close them all by saying,

"What more can he say than to you he hath said,
You who unto Jesus for refuge hath fled?"

Away then with dark suspicions and anxieties! Is it care about past sin? "The blood of Jesus Christ, God's dear Son, cleanseth us from all sin." Is it present temptation? "There hath no temptation happened to you but such as is common to men: but God who is faithful, who will not suffer you to be tempted above that ye are able; but will with the temptation also make a way to escape, that ye may be able to bear it." Is it future peril? O leave thou that with him, for neither "things present, nor things to come, nor height, nor depth, nor any other creature, shall be able to separate us from the love of God, which is in Christ Jesus our Lord." If you begin to think always of yourself, you must be miserable. Why, it is Christ that makes you what you are before the eyes of God; look then to Jesus in order to find out what you are in God's esteem. Soul, I say again look at Christ, and not at yourself. Never let anxieties about sanctification destroy your confidence of justification. What if you be a sinner! Christ died to save sinners. What if you be undeserving! "In due time Christ died for the ungodly." Grace is free. The invitation is still open to you; rest the whole burden of your soul's salvation where it must rest. Do not be an Uzza, lay no hasty hand upon the ark of the Lord; above all, do not be an Uzziah, attempt not to offer sacrifices or usurp the priesthood, for Christ must stand for you, you cannot stand or do for yourself. Cast, then, your care on him, for he careth for you.

I shall want your patient attention two or three minutes more, while trying to apply this remedy, when I notice that there are many cares not of a personal but rather of an *ecclesiastical* character, which often insinuate themselves and plead for life, but which must nevertheless be put away. I am sorry to confess, that if I do not preach to any one else this morning, I shall now be preaching to myself. There are cares about *how God's work is to be carried on*. I know a foolish young man who lies awake many nights thinking about that, and who sometimes by day makes himself foolishly sad, because with large purposes of heart and with great designs in his soul he sees not the way by which they are to be carried out, and has not yet attained the faith which

"Laughs at impossibilities,
And says, 'It shall be done.' "

If any of you are suffering from the same sad disease, let me exhort you from the words of Peter, to cast the care about God's work *upon God*. He never sent us a warfare at our own charge; he never did require us to do *his* work; that he will attend to himself; and we ought to feel that if God does not enable us to do as much as we would, it is a blessed thing to be enabled and permitted to do as much as we can. If we think there are few men to work, or little means with which to work, we must not be fretful about where the means, or the men shall come from. We may properly pray, "Lord, send labourers," and with equal propriety we may ask that he who has the silver and the gold, may give them for his own work; but after that we must cast our care on God. Then, if we get over that, there will be another anxiety,—one which frets me often enough—which is, *the success of God's work*. Oh! when there are souls converted, how our heart leaps for joy; when the Church keeps continually increasing, how glad we are! But if there is even a little lull, we feel so sad; if we do not see God's arm always bare, we are ready to lie down and say, "Lord, let me die, I am no better than my fathers." When we are in a low state of body and heart too, that weakening sickness of unbelief, like the woman's issue of blood, comes over us, and we feel that life is ebbing as success decreases. Now, this is a care we must cast on God. Husbandman, your Great Employer sent you out to sow the seed, but if no grain of it should ever come up, if you sowed the seed as he told you, and where he told you, he will never lay the blame of a defective harvest to you. It is ours to preach, but to convert souls is God's; it is ours to labour, but the success depends alone on him. "They that go through the valley of Baca make it a well,"—that is *their* business, to dig wells—"the rain also filleth the pools,"—it is not their business to fill the wells; and the wells do not get full from the bottom as they do in our country, it is the rain that fills the pools,—the blessing comes from on high; and if we have dug the wells, and we have prayed six times, and as yet the rain has not descended, go again seven times, and the rain shall yet descend, and the pools shall be filled to the brim. Do not, therefore, let us have cares about success.

And sometimes there is another care, it is the care lest some little slip made by ourselves or others should give cause to the enemy to blaspheme. There are devils besides those in hell, there are some on earth; and some of these are too glad to find an opportunity, if there be a word that is ever so fitly spoken, to wrest it out of its connection and make stock and capital for blasphemy out of it. It is an easy task and one which any fool can accomplish, but this world is full of fools who are glad to find dirt to eat, and then having eaten it themselves to cram it down others throats. One is sometimes afraid to walk for fear of breaking something in such a frail world as this; afraid to speak, lest we should say something which might open the enemy's mouth. A careful jealousy is very well if it leads to caution, but very ill if it leads to a carking, weak anxiety. What have you and I to do with what the enemy may do? if the Lord does not chain the devil I am sure we cannot, and if he does not shut the mouths of liars, I do not know that we ought to wish he would; for if he lets them open their mouths I have no doubt they are best open. Many a time, as Christ rode into Jerusalem on the back of an ass, the truth has ridden into the midst of Jerusalem in triumph on the back of its most despicable enemies. Beyond doubt, Christ has been lifted up even on the point of the spear, and the light of the gospel has beamed like a beacon from the stake where the martyr perished. Well, let us leave our enemies to do what they will, and only stand fast to the Lord and cast our care on him.

And then, one is so afraid of being unfaithful at the last, lest the blood of souls should be on our skirts. Oh! that thought has dashed me on my forehead on the floor many and many a time. This heavy burden crushes me into the most pitiable state, until the body sympathises with the mind so fully, that if you could see me with the tears running from my eyes, and the cold sweat starting from my head, you would say, "What a creature is that to go forth and preach." The thought of having all of you to address, and that I must be faithful or else your blood shall be required at my hands, is so awful a one that in private I never dare to think of it, for it utterly unmans me. But oh, blessed be God, if he has enabled us to do all we can by his Spirit, we must leave it there. We know that he will not ask more of us than he has given to us, and if he has helped us so far, his shall be the glory; but if we have failed, even that too shall be washed away through the precious blood, and with all his weight of responsibility the minister shall yet enter heaven and find a place amongst the sanctified.

### III. I close my last point upon which only a word, of the sweet inducement to leave your burden: "He careth for you."

Believe in an universal providence, the Lord cares for ants and angels, for worms and for worlds; he cares for cherubim and for sparrows, for seraphim and for insects.

Cast your care on him, he that calleth the stars by their names, and leadeth them out by numbers, by their hosts. "Why sayest thou, Oh Jacob, and thinkest Oh Israel, my way is passed over from God and he has utterly forgotten me?" Let his universal providence cheer you. Think next of his particular providence over all the saints. "Precious shall their blood be in his sight." "Precious in the sight of the Lord is the death of his saints." "We know that all things work together for good to them that love God, to them that are the called according to his purpose." Let the fact that while he is the Saviour of all men, he is specially the Saviour of them that believe, let that cheer and comfort you, that special providence which watches over the chosen, "The angel of the Lord encampeth round about them that fear him." And then, thirdly, let the thought of his special love *to you* be the very essence of your comfort. "I will never leave *thee*, nor forsake *thee*." God says, that as much to you, as he said it to any saint of old. "Fear not, I am thy shield, and thy exceeding great reward." Oh! I would beloved, that the Holy Ghost would make you feel the promise as being spoken to *you;* out of this vast assembly forget the rest and only think of yourself, for the promises are unto you, meant for you. Oh! grasp them. It is ill to get into a way of reading Scripture for the whole Church, read it for yourselves, and specially hear the Master say to you this morning, "Let not *your* heart be troubled, ye believe in God, believe also in me." Think that ye hear him say, "I have prayed for *thee* that thy faith fail not." Think thou seest him walking on the waters of thy trouble, for he is there and he is saying, "Fear not, it is I, be not afraid." Oh! those sweet words of Christ! Lord speak them to me; speak them to thy poor sorrowing child yonder; speak them to each one of us; speak them to us, and let us hear thy voice and say, "Jesus whispers consolation, I cannot refuse it, I will sit under his shadow with great delight."

Sinners, ungodly persons here, you know not God. I

send you away when I have said this one thing. What a blessed thing it is to be a Christian, to have some one who will take your cares for you! Why, you know you will have your cares whether you are Christians or not you are sure to have troubles even in the world, but then you have no Christ! to comfort you, no God to sustain you, no promise to cheer you; you have the darkness without the lamp, you have to die without the immortality to follow. Oh that you knew what a Christian is, and your mouths would be a watering to know the Christian's privilege. But I say to you, cast your sins upon Christ. Jesus Christ can take them. If thou believest on him there is proof that *he did* take them of old, did carry them and suffered for them in his own person that thou mightest go free. Oh may we each this morning, saint and sinner, come even to the cross, and to the throne of grace, and say, "Lord, unload us of our burdens of guilt and care, and give us now to go on our way rejoicing," because God, all-sufficient, has said, "I will never leave thee nor forsake thee."

# 2

# ANXIETY, AMBITION, INDECISION

*"Neither be ye of doubtful mind."*
*—Luke 12:29*

*"A hurricane of afflictions may beat about you, yet you*
*shall be a blessed man, for all the elements of blessedness*
*are within your own heart. God has given them to you,*
*and the devil himself cannot take them away."*

~

The chief concern of a man should be, to see that his own soul is right in the sight of God. Solomon said, "Keep thy heart with all diligence; for out of it are the issues of life." Many persons think a great deal about the adorning of the body, but do not think anything about the ornaments of the soul. The feeding of the physical frame engrosses much care, but the supply of spiritual food is often neglected. Yet, O man, thou thyself art better than thy body! Thine immortal soul is worth far more than that poor carcase of thine which will soon become food for worms; and all the things that thou hast, what are they compared with thine inner self,—thy real self,—thy heart, thy soul, thy spirit?

In our text, our Saviour bids us see to the condition of our mind: "Neither be ye of doubtful mind." He thus calls our attention to the higher and nobler part of our being, and bids us see to it that it is in a right state. No doubt there are some people who are in easier circumstances than others,—some who are in positions where they enjoy many comforts, while others are in places where they suffer many hardships; but, after all, happiness lies more in the mind than it does in the circumstances in which any individual is found, and the man within has far more to do with his own joy or sorrow than anything outside of him has. There have been some who have been perfectly free in a prison, while others have been in absolute bondage with wide estates to roam over. We have known some, whose spirits have triumphed when all around has tended to depress them; and we have seen others, who were wretched and desponding when they had, apparently, all that heart could wish. It is the mind which is the main thing; it will bring thee daylight or midnight, wealth or poverty, peace or war. I wish, dear friends, that half the time we spend in trying to better our circumstances were spent in bettering ourselves after the right fashion; and that even a tenth of the trouble we take to fit our circumstances to our desires were used in fitting our desires to our circumstances. If we did that, how much happier men and women we should be! Try as you may, you cannot alter the world in which your lot is cast, and you cannot alter God's providential arrangements; so, would it not be better that you should be altered so as to suit the providence, and be resigned to the will of God? It is beautiful to see how often the inspired writers of Holy Scripture were busy with what I may call indoor work,— the work that has to be done within one's own heart. "Bless the Lord, O my soul," says David, in the 103rd Psalm; "and all that is within me, bless his holy name." This indoor work, brethren and sisters in Christ, will always pay us best; and our Lord Jesus, in his exhortations, often bids us attend to it. Did he not say to his disciples, "Let not your heart be troubled"? A little later, he said to them, "In the world ye shall have tribulation;" and he says the same to his disciples in every age. It is no use for you to try to avoid that, for you will have tribulation; yet, "Let not your heart be troubled." All the water in the sea will not hurt your vessel so long as you keep it outside; the danger begins when it gets inside the ship. So, it matters little what is outside you, if all is right within. Have that little bird in your bosom that sings sweetly of the love of God; wear the flower called heart's-ease in your button-hole; and you may go merrily through a perfect wilderness of trouble and a desert of care. A hurricane of afflictions may beat about you, yet you shall be a blessed man, for all the elements of blessedness are within your own heart. God has given them to you, and the devil himself cannot take them away.

In speaking upon this text, I mean to preach a good part of the sermon to myself, for I need it as much as anybody does; but I ask each brother and sister to take home to themselves any part that suits them. And before I have done, I shall have a word for you unconverted people, and I pray God that that word may do you good, and that you may cease to be of a doubtful mind. The original of the text is not easy to explain, for the word translated "doubtful" is not used anywhere else in the New Testament. It appears to have something to do with meteors, so that the passage might be rendered, "Neither be ye of meteoric mind."

As the word is so singular, there have been a great many different opinions as to its meaning. Some have said that it relates to high things that float above, such as the clouds. If they are right, our text says to us, "Do not be like the clouds,—do not have cloudy minds, blown about with every wind of doctrine." Others render it, "Do not be like the birds, high up in the air, always on the wing, unsettled and uncertain, ever flying about, and never at rest." Others find an allusion to the ship that is far out upon the sea, and the text says to them, "Do not always be at sea, tossed up and down; have some anchorage; do not be always drifting to and fro." The word "doubtful" means so much that I do not expect to be able to tell you all that it means, but shall rather give you a few practical thoughts concerning it.

## 1. "Neither be ye of doubtful mind." That is, first, children of God, be not anxious. Be not tossed up and down by your outward circumstances.

If God prospers you, do not ride high, as the vessel does when the tide lifts it up; and if he does not prosper you, do not sink down as the vessel does when the tide ebbs away again. Do not be so affected by external things as to get into a state of worry, and fretfulness, and care, and anxiety, and distress.

Our Saviour's injunction means, "Do not be anxious about your temporal affairs." Be prudent; you have no right to spend the money of other people, nor yet your own, in wastefulness. You are to be careful and discreet, for every Christian should remember that he is only a steward, and that he is accountable to his Master for whatever he has, and the use he makes of it. But when you have done your best with your little, do not worry because you cannot make it more. And when you have done your best to meet your expenses, do not sit down, and wring your hands because you cannot lessen them. You cannot make a shilling into a sovereign, but be thankful if you have the shilling; and if you sometimes find that you must live from hand to mouth, recollect that you are not the first child of God who has had his manna every morning, nor the first of God's servants to have bread and flesh in the morning, and bread and flesh in the evening, with nothing to lay by for the morrow. If this is your case, be not staggered and astonished, as though some new thing had happened unto you; and do not begin to fret, and fume, and worry, and trouble yourself about what you cannot help. Can you alter it with all your worrying?

Have you,—you who are in the habit of worrying and fretting,—ever made any profit by doing so? How much a year do you think that anybody would give you for all your fretting? How much has it brought you in? Come, brother, if it is a good business, I would like to go into partnership with you; but I should like first to know something about your profits. As I look at your face, I notice that it is careworn and anxious. That does not seem to indicate that the business is a profitable one. If I listen to your speech, I hear you murmuring a great deal instead of praising God. That does not seem to me to be a profitable concern. In fact, as far as I have ascertained, either by my own experience or by the observation of others, I have never discovered that anxiety has comforted anybody, or that it has brought any grist to the mill, or any meal to the barrel. Well, if a thing does not pay, what is the good of it?

But perhaps you say, "I cannot help fretting and worrying." No, my good brother or sister, but do you not think that the Lord can help you to help it, and that your faith in him, if it were what it ought to be, would soon be the end of your distress and trouble? Have you not found out yet—I have,—that the very anxiety, which arises through your being in a difficulty, unfits you to meet that difficulty? You are in a great hurry to do something or other, and that something or other does more mischief than could possibly have happened if you had kept still, resting in the Lord, and waiting patiently for him. Instead of doing so, you rush this way, and that way, and so add to your worries instead of decreasing them. You are like the servant with the basket of eggs on her head, who shakes her head because she is afraid her eggs will fall, and makes them fall by the very process of her trembling. So, you go and make ten troubles in endeavouring to get out of one.

There is a text that is very easy to repeat, but not always so easy to obey: "Stand still, and see the salvation of God." But you want to see your own salvation, so you cannot stand still. There is many a man who has run before God's cloud, and who has been very glad to run or even to crawl back again. Some people are so anxious to carve for themselves that they cut their own fingers; they had better leave the carving in the hands of God, and take what he gives them, for he knows far better than they do what is good for them, and his hand is infinitely wiser than theirs can possibly be.

"Oh, but!" says one, "I feel that I must be doing something." That "doing" will just be your undoing unless you stop and consider what God would have you do. The probability is that your action will be unwise and hasty while you are in your present feverish condition. Wait till you get quite cool, brother; you will see your way far better then. At the present moment, you are in such a fidget and flutter that you are very apt to mistake your right hand for your left, and to put bitter for sweet, and sweet for bitter.

You say again that you cannot help being anxious. Then, my dear friend, I must very solemnly ask you what is the difference between you and the man of the world? There is an orphan child, and it is afraid it will not be fed; but you have a Father in heaven, and if you are afraid, surely, it is of little use for you to have such a Father. Are you not dishonouring his holy name by such conduct as that? Do you not think that others, who see you in this condition, will say, "There is not much power in religion, for these people, who profess to be Christians, are not comforted by it in their time of trouble, and it will not be of much use to them in the hour of their death." Remember Jeremiah's questions, "If thou hast run with the footmen, and they have wearied thee, then how canst thou contend with horses? and if in the land of peace, wherein thou trustest, they wearied thee, then how wilt thou do in the swelling of Jordan?" Surely it is time that we plucked up courage, and were not so easily disheartened, for we have worse trials on ahead than any we have yet been called to endure.

"That is just what I dread," says one. What would you do, then, brother? "I have been thinking that perhaps I had better turn back." But you have no armour for your back; and the perils of going back are far worse than the perils of going forward. Therefore, I charge thee, if thou art indeed a believer in the Lord Jesus Christ, to play the man, and let thy faith overcome thy fear. Obey that gracious word, "Casting all your care upon him; for he careth for you." Do you not believe that "all things work together for good to them that love God, to them who are the called according to his purpose"? You say that you do. Do you not believe that—

"He sits a Sovereign on his throne
And ruleth all things well"?

You say that you do. Do you not believe he loves you with an everlasting love? Do you not know that he spared not his only-begotten Son, but delivered him up for you; and do you think that, after having done so much for you, he will withhold from you anything that is necessary for your well-being? You must not think so. Brother, sister, it would be unkind, ungenerous, ungrateful to think so. Therefore, be not of anxious or doubtful mind concerning temporal things.

"Well," says one, "as far as temporal supplies are concerned, I can leave them entirely in the hands of God; but my anxieties arise from quite another form of trouble. There is a Christian brother who is at enmity against me, and he has been spreading an ill report about me, although I have earnestly sought to walk before God in holy fear, and have watched every step that I have taken, and I feel so worried that I do not know what to do." Well, dear friend, there is one rule which you will generally find to be applicable in such a case as yours. When you do not know what to do, do not do anything at all; and, usually, if the trouble has arisen through false reports about your own character, "the least said, the soonest mended." I believe that, if there is anything you want to have well done, you had better do it yourself; but there is one exception to that rule, and that is the matter of defending yourself. No defence is needed for a good man who can say, "By the grace of God I am what I am." You may leave that matter of your own character, therefore; and as to the good brother not getting on with you, if you have done anything that has grieved him, confess the wrong. "Well, perhaps, if I did, he might not meet me in the same spirit." You have nothing to do with that, dear friend; that is his business, and God's. You go and do the right thing, and then be no longer anxious about it, but leave the result with God.

I hear another brother say, "My anxiety has nothing to do with my personal affairs; I am anxious about the cause of God,—the church over which I preside,—the Bible-class that I conduct,—the mission-field that I try to cultivate. Somehow, things do not go as I could wish, and I am greatly concerned that they are not more prosperous." And what are you doing, good friend, to bring about that result? Are you telling the Lord about it, and agonizing before him in prayer? That is right; but if you are telling yourself about it, and your anxiety is confined to yourself, no good will come of that. "But, sir, all things seem to be going amiss." Yes, I am constantly hearing that. There are some of our friends who believe that we have fallen upon the worst days that have ever been known in this world. Well, it may be so, I cannot say much about that; but I will say this, my dear friends,—that you and I are not of anything like so much importance to the Church of God as we may have imagined; and that the particular department of work which has been entrusted to us, though we ought to think well of it, and to do it well, is not, after all, the hinge upon which the whole universe turns. God managed the world very well before we were born, and he will manage it quite as well when we are dead;

his Church will not die, for the Lord still liveth, and his Spirit still abides in the Church, and therefore it must live.

But there will be trouble for us if we begin to think that everything depends upon us. Uzzah was well intentioned, no doubt; yet God smote him for putting forth his hand to stay the ark of the Lord from falling. Let none of us become guilty of Uzzah's sin. It is our business to serve the Lord with all our heart and soul, just as Martha, with all her energy, sought to prepare a supper for Jesus; but when we begin to be cumbered about our service, then we may expect the Master to say to us, as he did to Martha, "Thou art careful and troubled about many things: but one thing is needful; and Mary hath chosen that good part, which shall not be taken away from her." It is not well that we should be cumbered about our service. No, brethren; the Lord loves his Church far better than we do, and he knows far better than we do how to manage her affairs, so we must—

"Just do the little we can do,

And leave the rest with him."

May his blessed Spirit help us so to get rid of all improper anxieties!

**II. Another meaning of the text will make a second division of our subject. "Be not ambitious." That is, do not fly high; do not be as the clouds and the meteors, that not only move about, and are uncertain in their movements, but are also high and lofty.**

Some people are troubled because they are *aiming at amassing great wealth*. Years ago, if anybody had told them they would one day possess what they have already obtained, they would have thought it was a wonderful sum, more than sufficient to satisfy all their desires. If somebody had asked them, "Will you retire from business then, and be quite happy and content?" they would have answered, "Oh, yes, certainly!" Well, they have gathered far more than that already, yet they are as grasping as ever, and they want more, and more, and more, and they are by no means content with what they have, much as it is. We should all be happier than we are if we were more contented with what is really all that we need, namely, having food and raiment, having neither poverty nor riches. Many men have been like that dog, in the fable, that had the meat in his mouth, but did not eat it because he saw the shadow of it in the water, and was so anxious to get that shadow as well as the substance that he already had that he lost the piece that he might have eaten. Such people are always trying to grasp the shadow, instead of enjoying what God has given to them. Let us not be of such a mind as that.

There are others, who are *ambitious to attain a higher position.* They might be very well content with the kind, good friends they have, but there was a lord, who once looked at them; and ever since that time, they have thought it a very wonderful thing to know a real, live lord. I have heard of a man who used to boast that the king once spoke to him; and though his majesty only told him to get out of the way, he was very proud of having been addressed by the king; and there are many people who think a great deal of that sort of thing. They are only shillings now, but they are anxious to get among the sovereigns. I have no sympathy with that desire; the best society in the world for me is a company of the Lord's people; and whether they are poor or rich, so long as they are God's saints, I feel myself at home with them. If a brother spoils the Queen's English, and makes a great many mistakes in pronunciation, that does not matter to me. The real piety that is in the man, the grace of God that is in his soul,—that is the thing which ought to please us. To be proud of our association with the great ones of the earth, is both a folly and a sin on the part of any child of God.

Sometimes, we are *ambitious in the service of God beyond*

*what we ought to be.* You are doing well in that little chapel, my brother; the place is full, and God is blessing you; but you want a bigger place, or you want to get away from those poor people whom the Lord has helped through your ministry. Possibly, my friend, you are a Sunday-school teacher, and you have charge of the infants, and they love you, and you are fitted for the work; yet you are not content to be an infant-class teacher, you would like a senior class, and a great stupid you would make of yourself, if you had such a class, for you are not adapted for it. It is well always to be seeking to do more for the Lord Jesus Christ, but I would earnestly discourage you from endeavouring to attain to a higher position merely for the sake of occupying it. Dear brethren and sisters, be not ambitious in this sense; for, after all, what is human greatness? Have you ever met with a really great man who would have given a penny for his own greatness? Do you not know that the higher you rise, even in the Church of Christ, the more responsibility you have, and the heavier burdens you have to carry? Do you not also know that the way to be really great is to be little, and that he who is greatest of all is the one who has learned to be least of all? He who is chief in the Church of Christ is he who serves the Church most, and who is willing to go lowest for Christ's sake. Cultivate that kind of greatness as much as you like; but put aside the other, and be not of ambitious mind even in your Lord's service.

I meet, every now and then, people who are, I hope, God's children, but they seem to me to have got into a very curious state of mind. They have notions, that are not at all according to the realities of every-day life,—flighty notions,—romantic notions about their own rights, and dignities, and importance, and so on. Ah, dear brethren and sisters, some of us were, in our own estimation, very important individuals, were we not, before the grace of God came into us? But when the grace of God works in us, we are made to feel that the very lowest and meanest place is a better position than we have any right to take. When we are in our right senses, we never give ourselves those high and mighty airs. A truly humble believer does not say, "So-and-so did not treat me with proper respect." Oh, dear me! what is the proper respect to which you and I are entitled? May the Lord preserve us from such a spirit as that! But there are some people,—professing Christians, too,—whose heads are always being filled with that kind of nonsense. They do not seem to have learned that the spirit of Christ is a spirit of meekness, which teaches us to bear and forbear, to forgive until seventy times seven, to expect to have our rights trampled on, and to be willing to lay them all down for any who please to tread upon them. It is blessed to feel, "I will be content to take any place, so long as I can love others, and do them good by loving them, so long as I can but love them to Christ, and help them to love Christ, and manifest the love of Christ to them." O brothers and sisters, we all need to go to school to our dear Lord and Master! You have never read that he said anything about his rights, or about defending his dignity. No, he who is the King of kings, and Lord of lords, was the servant of servants when he was here upon earth; and, truly, he that serves most is the most royal of all. Therefore, "let this mind be in you, which was also in Christ Jesus," and then you will not be anxious or ambitious to be great.

### III. A third meaning of the text is this, "Be ye not of irresolute mind, without decision of character."

If you look at the connection of the passage, you will see that this meaning fits in exceedingly well. There are persons, in the world, who may be described as time-servers. The main consideration with them is, what they shall eat, or what they shall drink, or how they shall be clothed; so they are always watching to see which is the best way to go in reference to those matters. As the old proverb has it, they know on which side their bread is buttered; or, according to another familiar saying, they are waiting to see which way the cat jumps; and when they have ascertained that, their "principles" will lead them to jump in that particular direction. Mr. John Bunyan, in "The Pilgrim's Progress," has well described just such persons,—Mr. By-ends and Mr. Fair-speech; and some of us have known their descendants. You remember hearing of the waterman, who got his living by looking one way, and pulling another; and that waterman has had a great many sons, of very much the same character as himself, and they have made a certain kind of progress in the world by that sort of scheming. But you and I, beloved, are not to be of irresolute mind. Every Christian should say, "By the grace of God, my mind is made up to serve him, cost what it may. Does my Lord desire me to keep the Sabbath day holy? Sunday is the best day in my particular line of business, but that does not matter to me. My mind is made up to serve the Lord; and whatever it costs, will make no difference to me. There is a party to be held to-night; and I know that, if I go to it, I shall have to witness the utmost frivolity, and I shall have to be a partaker in what will be, to me, a good deal of sin. Uncle Jonas will be angry if I don't go; but I mean to do the right thing, whether Uncle Jonas is pleased, or no." That is the way all you, who have the love of God shed abroad in your hearts, ought to speak. The question, "What is right?" being answered, you have only to do the right, whatever happens. This is what our Lord meant when he said to his disciples, "Neither be ye of doubtful mind."

"Oh, but!" say some, "we really must look at both sides of that question. There may come a time when we know that a certain course is right; but, if we take it, we may bring ruin upon ourselves. and upon others, too." Let me read the 4th and 5th verses of this chapter, and when I have done so, there will be no need for you to say anything: "Be not afraid of them that kill the body, and after that have no more that they can do. But I will forewarn you whom ye shall fear: Fear him, which after he hath killed hath power to cast into hell; yea, I say unto you, Fear him;" and the 8th and 9th verses: "Whosoever shall confess me before men, him shall the Son of man also confess before the angels of God: but he that denieth me before men shall be denied before the angels of God." Does not that decide you? God grant that it may, and that you may henceforth say, "I will confess Christ, and act for the right and the true; and, by the aid of his blessed Spirit I will never hesitate to do as he bids me.

" 'Through floods and flames, if Jesus lead,

I'll follow where He goes;'—

"neither will I be of doubtful mind."

## IV. A fourth meaning of the text is, "Be ye not at sea so far as your own personal salvation is concerned."

Brothers and sisters, *there are some, who are not saved, who yet imagine that they are.* There are many, who know nothing of vital godliness, yet who sing as joyfully as the brightest of saints, never suspecting their real condition in the sight of God. Whenever I meet with a man who never has had a doubt about his own condition, I feel inclined to quote to him those lines of Cowper,—

"He has no hope who never had a fear;

And he that never doubted of his state,

He may perhaps—perhaps he may—too late."

Beware of all presumption. There are some, who even decry anything like self-examination. They cannot bear for us to look for the signs and tokens of the Holy Spirit's work within them; and if we talk about practical holiness, they say that we are getting upon legal ground, and turning aside to the "beggarly elements" of the law. From all such turn away, for they can do you no good. You are exhorted, in the Scriptures, to examine yourselves, to see whether you are in the faith, and to prove your own selves; nay, self-examination alone is not sufficient, and you must cry, with the psalmist, "Search me, O God, and know my heart: try me, and know my thoughts: and see if there be any wicked way in me, and lead me in the way everlasting."

But, on the other hand, *there are some, who think, that doubts and fears are necessary to a child of God.* I draw a very grave distinction between doubting the truth of God's promise, and questioning whether that promise is made to me; they are two very different things. To doubt the power of the blood of Jesus Christ to cleanse from all sin, is one thing; but, sometimes, to question whether I really have trusted in that blood, is quite another thing. The first is sinful; the second is only proper and discreet. I would advise everyone often to look to the foundation of his faith, to see whether he really has believed in Jesus, and has, in his heart, the true life which grows out of such faith. But, brethren, there is really no reason in a man saying, "Whether I am a child of God, or not, I am sure I do not know; I sometimes hope I am;"—and so on. I suppose there are few men who have not, at some time or other, suffered pain; but it is not necessary for us always to have the toothache in order to prove that we really are men. And, in like manner, there are few Christians who have never had any doubts, yet it is not necessary to be always doubting in order to prove that we are Christians; but, as we are glad enough to get rid of pain, so are we to be glad to get rid of doubt by fully trusting our Lord who is so worthy of our trust. Dear brethren, you ought to know, you can know, you can know now, whether you are saved, or not. At any rate, if I did not know myself to be saved, I would give no sleep to my eyes, nor slumber to my eyelids, till I had found the Saviour. If a shadow of a doubt about my being washed in the blood of Christ were on my soul, I would get to my knees, and not rise from them until I did really know that Christ had saved me. If you are in doubt, and yet are content about your condition,

I fear that you know nothing at all about the matter; for the true child of God, if he is in any doubt about his salvation, is uneasy till that doubt is gone. He cannot rest till he knows that he is saved; and, after all, that is not a very difficult thing to know, for we are told, over and over again, in this blessed Book, that he that believeth in Christ is not condemned, but hath everlasting life. If you have believed in him, you are not condemned, you have his own word for it. He who trusts to Jesus only, builds on a sure foundation; so, if you are trusting in him, you may have the full assurance that you have passed from death unto life, and shall never come into condemnation. Do not, brother, go limping along all your life when you might run in the way of God's commandments. A good old minister, of my acquaintance, when people used to say to him that they hoped, and hoped, and never got any further than that, was in the habit of replying, "You are always hoping, and hopping; I hope you will learn to run one of these days,—to run without weariness in the ways of God."

The last thing I have to do is to bid all here present, who have not believed in the Lord Jesus Christ, to do so at once. My dear friends, my text says, "Neither be ye of doubtful mind." But you cannot help being of doubtful mind while you remain as you are, and I really wish that your conscience would trouble you even more than it now does,—that your uneasiness might become even greater, and your unrest yet more unrestful. Look at yourself, my dear hearer. You have not believed in Christ, so you are in debt to divine justice, and you are hopelessly bankrupt, for you cannot meet one in a million of the claims that are recorded against you; how can you rest as long as you are thus indebted to God? You are a prisoner, too. When Marshal Bazaine had many of the comforts of life on the Isle of St. Marguerite, off the coast of the South of France, he could not rest till he had regained his liberty; and I marvel how you can be so happy, even with the joys of this world, while you are without the great blessing of spiritual liberty. I wish you felt that you could not rest till you had become emancipated from the bondage of sin, and been made the Lord's freeman. How would you like to be in a condemned cell, and not to know when your execution was to take place? I am sure that you would pity any poor creature, whatever his crime, if you could see him under such circumstances. Perhaps you say that you are living in a wide world, and not in a prison; yet you are condemned already. It was said of the old Roman Empire that, if a man once broke the law, the whole world was a prison for him, for Cæsar had almost universal sway; and God sees you wherever you are, and everywhere you are in the condemned cell; and, perhaps, before the sun shall rise again, your execution will have taken place.

I have been told that, some years ago, there went into the chamber of horrors at Madame Tussaud's exhibition a young gentleman, who was foolish enough to put himself under the guillotine,—in the place which had been occupied by criminals; and as he lay there, with his bare neck exposed to the terrible knife, he was so struck with horror that he was unable to move; and people who went by thought he was one of the waxwork figures, and he could not stir until someone took him away. And, oh, if you did but know where you really are, with that dreadful axe of divine justice just above your head, you might well be paralyzed with horror! Only let your breath fail, or your pulse stop, and down it descends to your utter destruction. But, alas! you are insensible to these things. May the Spirit of God arouse you! May he make you feel your true position, and then I am sure you will not be content to remain a moment longer of a doubtful and undecided mind. Hearken, my friend. That sin of thine can be forgiven, for Jesus died for sinners. That heart of thine can be renewed by grace, for Jesus lives again. You can be delivered from the wrath to come, for Jesus has gone up on high to plead for just such sinners as you are. What are you to do in order that you may have Christ as your

Saviour? Why, as the hymn says,—
  "Only trust him, only trust him,
  Only trust him now."

# 3
# PRAYER, THE CURE FOR CARE

*"Be careful for nothing; but in every thing by prayer and supplication with thanksgiving let your requests be made known unto God. And the peace of God, which passeth all understanding, shall keep your hearts and minds through Christ Jesus."*
*—Philippians 4:6, 7*

*"Leave off, then, this damaging habit of worry and take to this enriching habit of prayer! See how you will thus make a double gain—first, by avoiding a loss, and secondly, by getting that which will really benefit you and others, too!"*

~

We have the faculty of forethought; but, like all our faculties, it has been perverted, and it is often abused. It is good for a man to have a holy care, and to pay due attention to every item of his life; but, alas! it is very easy to make it into an unholy care, and to try to wrest from the hand of God that office of providence which belongs to him and not to ourselves. How often Luther liked to talk about the birds, and the way God cares for them! When he was full of his anxieties, he used constantly to envy the birds because they led so free and happy a life. He talks of Dr. Sparrow, and Dr. Thrush, and others that used to come and talk to Dr. Luther, and tell him many a good thing. You know, brethren, the birds out in the open yonder, cared for by God, fare far better than those that are cared for by man. A little London girl, who had gone into the country, once said, "Look, mamma, at that poor little bird; it has not got any cage!" That would not have struck me as being any loss to the bird; and if you and I were without our cage, and the box of seed, and glass of water, it would not be much of a loss if we were cast adrift into the glorious liberty of a life of humble dependence upon God. It is that cage of carnal trust, and that box of seed that we are always labouring to fill, that makes the worry of this mortal life; but he who has grace to spread his wings and soar away, and get into the open field of divine trustfulness, may sing all the day, and ever have this for his tune,—

"Mortal, cease from toil and sorrow;

God provideth for the morrow."

Here, then, is the teaching of the text: "Be careful for nothing." The word "careful" does not now mean exactly what it did when the Bible was translated; at least, it conveys a different meaning to me from what it did to the translators. I would say that we should be careful. "Be careful," is a good lesson for boys and young people when they are starting in life; but, in the sense in which the word "care-ful" was understood at the time of the translators, we must not be careful, that is, full of care. The text means, be not anxious; be not constantly thinking about the needs of this mortal life. I will read it again, stretching the word out a little, and then you will get the meaning of it: "Be care-ful for nothing." Oh, that God might teach us how to avoid the evil which is here forbidden, and to live with that holy carelessness which is the very beauty of the Christian life, when all our care is cast on God, and we can joy and rejoice in his providential care of us!

"Ah!" says somebody, "I cannot help caring." Well, the subject to-night is to help you to leave off caring; and, first, consider here *the substitute for care*. Be careful for nothing, but be prayerful for everything; that is the substitute for care, "prayer and supplication." Secondly, note *the special character of this prayer*, which is to become the substitute for anxiety: "In every thing by prayer and supplication with thanksgiving let your requests be made known unto God." And then I hope we shall have a few minutes left in which to consider *the sweet effect of this prayer*: "The peace of God, which passeth all understanding, shall keep your hearts and minds through Christ Jesus."

## I. To begin, then, here is, first, the substitute for care.

I suppose it is true of many of us that *our cares are manifold*. If you once become careful, anxious, fretful, you will never be able to count your cares, even though you might count the hairs of your head. And cares are apt to multiply to those who are care-full; and when you are as full of care as you think you can be, you will be sure to have another crop of cares growing up all around you. The indulgence of this ill habit of anxiety leads to its getting dominion over life, till life is not worth living by reason of the care we have about it. Cares are manifold; therefore, let your prayers be as manifold. Turn into a prayer everything that is a care. Let your cares be the raw material of your prayers; and, as the alchemists hoped to turn dross into gold, so do you, by a holy alchemy, actually turn what naturally would have been a care into spiritual treasure in the form of prayer. Baptize every anxiety into the name of the Father, and of the Son, and of the Holy Ghost, and so make it into a blessing.

Have you a care to get? Take heed that it does not get you. Do you wish to make gain? Mind you do not lose more than you gain by your gains. I beseech you, have no more care to gain than you dare turn into a prayer. Do not desire to have what you dare not ask God to give you.

41

Measure your desires by a spiritual standard, and you will thus be kept from anything like covetousness. Cares come to many from their losses; they lose what they have gained. Well, this is a world in which there is the tendency to lose. Ebbs follow floods, and winters crush out summer flowers. Do not wonder if you lose as other people do; but pray about your losses. Go to God with them; and instead of fretting, make them an occasion for waiting upon the Lord, and saying, "The Lord gave, and the Lord hath taken away; blessed be the name of the Lord. Show me wherefore thou contendest with me, and deliver thy servant, I pray thee, from ever complaining of thee whatever thou dost permit me to lose!"

Perhaps you say that your care is neither about your gainings nor your losings, but even about your daily bread. Ah, well, you have promises for that, you know! The Lord has said, "So shalt thou dwell in the land, and verily thou shalt be fed." He gives you sweet encouragement when he says that he clothes the grass of the field, and shall he not much more clothe you, O ye of little faith? And the Lord Jesus bids you consider the fowls of heaven, how they sow not, neither do they gather into barns, and yet your heavenly Father feedeth them. Go, then, to your God with all your cares. If you have a large family, a slender income, and much ado to make ends meet, and to provide things honest in the sight of all men, you have so many excuses for knocking at God's door, so many more reasons for being often found at the throne of grace. I beseech you, turn them to good account. I feel free to call upon a friend when I really have some business to do with him; and you may be bold to call upon God when necessities press upon you. Instead of caring for anything with anxious care, turn it at once into a reason for renewed prayerfulness.

"Ah!" says one, "but I am in perplexity; I do not know what to do." Well, then, dear friend, you should certainly pray when you cannot tell whether it is the right hand road, or the left hand, or straight on, or whether you should go back. Indeed, when you are in such a fog that you cannot see the next lamp, then is the time that you must pray. The road will clear before you very suddenly. I have often had to try this plan myself; and I bear witness that, when I have trusted to myself, I have been a gigantic fool, but when I have trusted in God, then he has led me straight on in the right way, and there has been no mistake about it. I believe that God's children often make greater blunders over simple things than they do over more difficult matters. You know how it was with Israel, when those Gibeonites came, with their old shoes and clouted, and showed the bread that was mouldy, that they said they took fresh out of their ovens. The children of Israel thought, "This is a clear case; these men are strangers, they have come from a far country, and we may make a league with them." They were certain that the evidence of their eyes proved that these were no Canaanites, so they did not consult God; the whole matter seemed so plain that they made a league with the Gibeonites, which was a trouble to them ever afterwards. If we would in everything go to God in prayer, our perplexities would lead us into no more mistakes than our simplicities; and in simple things and difficult things we should be guided by the Most High.

Perhaps another friend says, "But I am thinking about the future." Are you? Well, first, I beg to ask you what you have to do with the future. Dost thou know what a day will bring forth? You have been thinking about what will become of you when you are old; but are you sure that you ever will be old? I did know one Christian woman who used to worry herself about how she would get buried. That question never troubled me; and there are many other matters about which we need not worry ourselves. You can always find a stick with which to beat a dog; and, if you want a care, you can generally find a care with which to beat your own souls; but that is a poor occupation for any of you. Instead of doing that, turn everything that might be a subject of care into a subject of prayer. It will not be long before you have a subject of care, so you will not be long without a subject of prayer. Strike out that word "care", and just write in the stead of it this word "prayer"; and then, though your cares are manifold, your prayers will also be manifold.

Note, next, dear friends, that *undue care is an intrusion into God's province.* It is making yourself the father of the household instead of being a child; it is making yourself the master instead of being a servant, for whom the master provides his rations. Now, if, instead of doing that, you will turn care into prayer, there will be no intrusion, for you may come to God in prayer without being charged with presumption. He invites you to pray; nay, here, by his servant, he bids you "in every thing by prayer and supplication with thanks giving let your requests be made known unto God."

Once more, *cares are of no use to us, and they cause us great damage.* If you were to worry as long as you wished, you could not make yourself an inch taller, or grow another hair on your head, or make one hair white or black. So the Saviour tells us; and he asks, if care fails in such little things, what can care do in the higher matters of providence? It cannot do anything. A farmer stood in his fields, and said, "I do not know what will happen to us all. The wheat will be destroyed if this rain keeps on; we shall not have any harvest at all unless we have some fine weather." He walked up and down, wringing his hands, and fretting, and making his whole household uncomfortable; but he did not produce one single gleam of sunlight by all his worrying, he could not puff any of the clouds away with all his petulant speech, nor could he stay a drop of rain with all his murmurings.

What is the good of it, then, to keep gnawing at your own heart, when you can get nothing by it? Besides, it weakens our power to help ourselves, and especially our power to glorify God. A care-full heart hinders us from judging rightly in many things. I have often used the illustration (I do not know a better) of taking a telescope, breathing on it with the hot breath of our anxiety, putting it to our eye, and then saying that we cannot see anything but clouds. Of course we cannot, and we never shall while we breathe upon it. If we were but calm, quiet, self-possessed, and God-possessed, we should do the right thing. We should be, as we say, "all there" in the time of difficulty. That man may expect to have presence of mind who has the presence of God. If we forget to pray, do you wonder that we are all in a fidget, and a worry, and we do the first thing that occurs to us, which is generally the worst thing, instead of waiting till we saw what should be done, and then trustfully and believingly doing it as in the sight of God? Care is injurious; but if you only turn this care into prayer, then every care will be a benefit to you.

Prayer is wonderful material for building up the spiritual fabric. We are ourselves edified by prayer; we grow in grace by prayer; and if we will but come to God every moment with petitions, we shall be fast-growing Christians. I said to one this morning, "Pray for me, it is a time of need;" and she replied, "I have done nothing else since I woke." I have made the same request of several others, and they have said that they have been praying for me. I felt so glad, not only for my own sake who had received benefit from their prayers, but for their sakes, because they are sure to grow thereby. When little birds keep flapping their wings, they are learning to fly. The sinews will get stronger, and the birds will quit the nest before long; that very wing-clapping is an education, and the attempting to pray, the groaning, the sighing, the crying, of a prayerful spirit, is itself a blessing. Leave off, then, this endamaging habit of care, and take to this enriching habit of prayer. See how you will thus make a double gain; first, by avoiding a loss, and secondly, by getting that which will really benefit you and others, too.

Then, again, *cares are the effect of forgetfulness of Christ's closeness to us*. Did you notice how the context runs? "The

Lord is at hand. Be careful for nothing." The Lord Jesus Christ has promised to come again, and he may come to-night; at any moment he may appear. So Paul writes, "The Lord is at hand. Be careful for nothing; but in every thing by prayer and supplication with thanksgiving let your requests be made known unto God." Oh, if we could but stand on this earth as upon a mere shadow, and live as those who will soon have done with this poor transient life, if we held every earthly thing with a very loose hand, then we should not be caring, and worrying, and fretting, but we should take to praying, for thus we should grasp the real, and the substantial, and plant our feet upon the invisible, which is, after all, the eternal! Oh, dear friends, let the text, which I have read to you over and over again, now drop into your hearts as a pebble falls into a mountain tarn, and as it enters let it make rings of comfort upon the very surface of your soul!

**II. Now we want to look into the text a little more closely to see, in the second place, the special character of this prayer. What sort of prayer is that which will ease us of care?**

Well, first, it is *a prayer which deals with everything.* "In every thing" "let your requests be made known unto God." You may pray about the smallest thing and about the greatest thing; you may not only pray for the Holy Spirit, but you may pray for a new pair of boots. You may go to God about the bread you eat, the water you drink, the raiment you wear, and pray to him about everything. Draw no line, and say, "So far is to be under the care of God." Dear me, then, what are you going to do with the rest of life? Is that to be lived under the withering blight of a sort of atheism? God forbid! Oh, that we might live in God as to the whole of our being, for our being is such that we cannot divide it! Our body, soul, and spirit are one, and while God leaves us in this world, and we have necessities which arise out of the condition of our bodies, we must bring our bodily necessities before God in prayer. And you will find that the great God will hear you in these matters. Say not that they are too little for him to notice; everything is little in comparison with him. When I think of what a great God he is, it seems to me that this poor little world of ours is just one insignificant grain of sand on the seashore of the universe, and not worth any notice at all. The whole earth is a mere speck in the great world of nature; and if God condescends to consider it, he may as well stoop a little lower, and consider us; and he does so, for he says, "Even the very hairs of your head are all numbered." Therefore, in everything let your requests be made known unto God.

The kind of prayer that saves us from care is *prayer that is repeated*: "In every thing by prayer and supplication." Pray to God, and then pray again: "by prayer and supplication." If the Lord does not answer you the first time, be very grateful that you have a good reason for praying again. If he does not grant your request the second time, believe that he loves you so much that he wants to hear your voice again; and if he keeps you waiting till you have gone to him seven times, say to yourself, "Now I know that I worship the God of Elijah, for Elijah's God let him go again seven times before the blessing was given." Count it an honour to be permitted to wrestle with the angel. This is the way God makes his princes. Jacob had never been Israel if he had obtained the blessing from the angel at the first asking; but when he had to keep on wrestling till he prevailed, then he became a prince with God. The prayer that kills care is prayer that is continued and importunate.

Next, it is *intelligent prayer*: "Let your requests be made known unto God." I heard of a Mohammedan who spent, I think, six hours in prayer each day; and lest he should go to sleep, when on board a boat, he stood upright, and only had a rope stretched across, so that he might lean against it, and if he slept, he would fall. His object was to keep on for six hours with what he called prayer. "Well," I said to one who knew him, and who had seen him on board his dahabeah on the Nile, "What sort of prayer was it?" "Why," my friend replied, "he kept on repeating, 'There is no God but God, and Mohammed is the prophet of God,' the same thing over, and over, and over again." I said, "Did he ask for anything?" "Oh, no!" "Was he pleading with God to give him anything?" "No, he simply kept on with that perpetual repetition of certain words, just as a witch might repeat a charm." Do you think there is anything in that style of praying? And if you go on your knees, and simply repeat a certain formula, it will be only a mouthful of words. What does God care about that kind of praying? "Let your requests be made known unto God." That is true prayer. God does know what your requests are; but you are to pray to him as if he did not know. You are to make known your requests, not because the Lord does not know, but perhaps because you do not know; and when you have made your requests known to him, as the text tells you, you will more clearly have made them known to yourself. When you have asked intelligently, knowing what you have asked, and knowing why you have asked it, you will perhaps stop, and say to yourself, "No, I must not, after all, make that request." Sometimes, when you have gone on praying for what God does not give you, it may be that there will steal over your mind the conviction that you are not on the right track; and that result of your prayer will in itself do you good, and be a blessing to you.

But you are to pray, making your requests known unto God. That is, in plain English, say what you want; for this is true prayer. Get alone, and tell the Lord what you want; pour out your heart before him. Do not imagine that God wants any fine language. No, you need not run upstairs for your prayer-book, and turn to a collect; you will be a long time before you find any collect that will fit you if you are really praying. Pray for what you want just as if you were telling your mother or your dearest friend what your need is. Go to God in that fashion, for that is real prayer, and that is the kind of prayer that will drive away your care.

So, dear friends, again, the kind of prayer that brings freedom from care is *communion with God*. If you have not spoken to God, you have not really prayed. A little child has been known (I daresay your children have done it) to go and put a letter down the grating of a drain; and of course there was never any reply to a letter posted in that way. If the letter is not put into the post-box, so that it goes to the person to whom it is addressed, what is the use of it? So, prayer is real communication with God. You must realize that he is, and that he is the Rewarder of them that diligently seek him, or else you cannot pray. He must be a reality to you, a living reality; and you must believe that he does hear prayer, and then you must speak with him, and believe that you have the petition that you ask of him, and so you shall have it. He has never yet failed to honour believing prayer. He may keep you waiting for a while; but delays are not denials, and he has often answered a prayer that asked for silver by giving gold. He may have denied earthly treasure, but he has given heavenly riches of ten thousand times the worth, and the suppliant has been more than satisfied with the exchange. "Let your requests be made known unto God." I know what you do when you are in trouble; you go to your neighbour, but your neighbour does not want to see you quite so often about such business. Possibly you go to your brother; but there is a text that warns you not to go into your brother's house in the day of your calamity. You may call on a friend too often when you are hard up; he may be very pleased to see you till he hears what you are after; but if you go to your God, he will never give you the cold shoulder; he will never say that you come too often. On the contrary, he will even chide you because you do not come to him often enough.

There is one word which I passed over just now

because I wanted to leave it for my last observation on this point: "By prayer and supplication *with thanksgiving* let your requests be made known unto God." Now what does that mean? It means that the kind of prayer that kills care is *a prayer that asks cheerfully, joyfully, thankfully.* "Lord, I am poor; let me bless thee for my poverty, and then, O Lord, wilt thou not supply all my needs?" That is the way to pray. "Lord, I am ill; I bless thee for this affliction, for I am sure that it means some good thing to me. Now be pleased to heal me, I beseech thee!" "Lord, I am in a great trouble; but I praise thee for the trouble, for I know that it contains a blessing though the envelope is black-edged; and then, Lord, help me through my trouble!" That is the kind of prayer that kills care: "supplication with thanksgiving." Mix these two things well; one drachm,—no, two drachms of prayer, prayer and supplication, then one drachm of thanksgiving. Rub them well together, and they will make a blessed cure for care. May the Lord teach us to practise this holy art of the apothecary!

**III. I finish with this third point, the sweet effect of this prayer: "And the peace of God, which passeth all understanding, shall keep your hearts and minds through Christ Jesus."**

If you can pray in this fashion, instead of indulging evil anxiety, the result will be that *an unusual peace* will steal over your heart and mind, unusual, for it will be "the peace of God." What is God's peace? The unruffled serenity of the infinitely-happy God, the eternal composure of the absolutely well-contented God. This shall possess your heart and mind. Notice how Paul describes it: "The peace of God, which passeth all understanding." Other people will not understand it; they will not be able to make out how you can be so quiet. What is more, you will not be able to tell them; for if it surpasses all understanding, it certainly passes all expression; and what is even more wonderful, you will not understand it yourself.

It will be such a peace that it will be to you *unfathomable and immeasurable*. When one of the martyrs was about to burn for Christ, he said to the judge who was giving orders to fire the pile, "Will you come and lay your hand on my heart?" The judge did so. "Does it beat fast?" enquired the martyr. "Do I show any sign of fear?" "No," said the judge. "Now lay your hand on your own heart, and see whether you are not more excited than I am." Think of that man of God, who, on the morning he was to be burned, was so soundly asleep that they had to shake him to wake him; he had to get up to be burned, and yet knowing that it was to be so, he had such confidence in God that he slept sweetly. This is "the peace of God, which passeth all understanding." In those old Diocletian persecutions, when the martyrs came into the amphitheatre to be torn by wild beasts, when one was set in a red-hot iron chair, another was smeared with honey, to be stung to death by wasps and bees, they never flinched. Think of that brave man who was put on a gridiron to be roasted to death, and who said to his persecutors, "You have done me on one side; now turn me over to the other." Why this peace under such circumstances? It was "the peace of God, which passeth all understanding." We do not have to suffer like that nowadays; but if it ever comes to anything like that, it is wonderful what peace a Christian enjoys. After there had been a great storm, the Master stood up in the prow of the vessel, and said to the winds, "Be still," and "there was a great calm," we read. Have you ever felt this? You do feel it to-night if you have learnt this sacred art of making your requests known unto God in everything, and the peace of God which passeth all understanding is keeping your hearts and minds through Christ Jesus.

This blessed peace keeps our hearts and minds; it is *a guardian peace*. The Greek word implies a garrison. Is it not an odd thing that a military term is used here, and that it is peace that acts as a guard to the heart and to the mind? It is the peace of God that is to protect the child of God; strange but beautiful figure! I have heard that fear is the housekeeper for a Christian. Well, fear may be a good guardian to keep dogs out; but it has not a full cupboard. But peace, though it seems weakness, is the essence of strength; and, while it guards, it also feeds us, and supplies all our needs.

It is also *a peace which links us to Jesus:* "The peace of God which passeth all understanding, shall keep your hearts and minds,"—that is, your affections and your thoughts, your desires and your intellect; your heart, so that it shall not fear; your mind, so that it shall not know any kind of perplexity;—"the peace of God shall keep your hearts and minds through Christ Jesus." It is all "through Christ Jesus," and therefore it is doubly sweet and precious to us.

O my dear hearers, some of you come in here on Thursday nights, and you do not know anything about this peace of God, and perhaps you wonder why we Christian people make such a fuss about our religion. Ah, if you knew it, you would perhaps make more fuss about it than we do; for if there were no hereafter,—and we know that there is,—yet the blessed habit of going to God in prayer, and casting all our care upon him, helps us to live most joyfully even in this life. We do not believe in secularism; but if we did, there would be no preparation for the earthly life like this living unto God, and living in God. If you have a sham god, and you merely go to church or chapel, and carry your prayer-book or your hymn-book with you, and therefore think you are Christians, you are deceiving yourselves; but if you have a living God, and you have real fellowship with him, and constantly, as a habit, live beneath the shadow of the wings of the Almighty, then you shall enjoy a peace that shall make others wonder, and make you yourself marvel, too, even "the peace of God, which passeth all understanding." God grant it to you, my beloved hearers, for Christ's sake! Amen.

4

# THE JEWEL OF PEACE

*"Now the Lord of peace himself give you peace always by all*
*means. The Lord be with you all."*
*—2 Thessalonians 3:16.*

*"You do not know the gospel, dear friends,*
*if you have not obtained peace through it;*
*peace is the juice, the essence, the soul of the gospel."*

~

When the heart is full of love it finds the hand too feeble for its desires. Hence it seeks relief in intercession and benediction; wishing, praying and blessing where it cannot actually effect its loving purpose. The apostle would have done for the Thessalonians all the good that was conceivable had it been in his power, but his wishes far outstripped his abilities, and therefore he betook himself to interceding for them, and to invoking upon them the blessing of the Lord and Master whom he served. Here is a lesson for us in the art of doing good; as we lengthen the eyesight with the telescope, as we send our words afar by the telegraph, so let us extend our ability to do good by the constant use of intercessory prayer. Parents, when you have done all you can for your children yourselves, be thankful that you may introduce them to a further and greater blessing, by commending them to the care of the great Father in heaven. Friends, do your friends the best possible deed of friendship by asking for them the friendship of God. You who love the souls of men, when you have poured out all your strength on their behalf, bless God that there is still something more which you can do, for by earnest entreaties and supplications you may bring down from on high the effectual energy of the Holy Spirit, who can work in their hearts that which it is not in your power to accomplish. The apostle saw that the Thessalonians were much troubled, and he wrote the most encouraging words to cheer them, but he knew that he could not take the burden from off their hearts, and therefore he turned to the God of all consolation, and prayed him to give them peace always by all means. The slenderness of our power to bless others will be no detriment to them if it lead us to lay hold upon the eternal strength, for that will bring into the field a superior power to bless, and our infirmity will only make space for the display of divine grace.

Let us look first at *the many-sided blessing* which the apostle invokes,—peace; and then let us note *the special desirableness of it.* Thirdly, let us observe *from whom alone it comes*; and fourthly, note *the wide sweep of the apostolic prayer.*

## I. First, then, let us look at the many-sided blessing,—"The Lord of peace himself give you peace."

Some have thought to restrict the expression to peace within the church, since disorderly members were evidently increasing among the Thessalonians; but that is a very straitened and niggardly interpretation, and it is never wise to narrow the meaning of God's word. Indeed, such a contracted explanation cannot be borne, for it does not appear that the disorderly persons mentioned in the chapter had as yet created any special disturbance: they had been quietly fattening at the expense of their generous brethren and would not be very eager to quarrel with the rack from which they fed. Although no doubt church quiet is included as one variety of peace, yet it would be a sad dwarfing of the meaning of the Spirit to consider one phase of the blessing to the neglect of the rest. No, the peace here meant is "the deep tranquillity of a soul resting on God," the quiet restfulness of spirit which is the peculiar gift of God, and the choice privilege of the believer. "Great peace have all they that love thy law, and nothing shall offend them."

The peace of the text is a gem with many facets, but in considering its many-sidedness we must remember that its main bearing is *toward God.* The deepest, best, and most worthy peace of the soul is its rest towards the Lord God himself. I trust we know this, and are enjoying it at this moment. We are no longer afraid of God: the sin which divided us from him is blotted out, and the distance which it created has ceased to be. The atonement has wrought perfect reconciliation and established everlasting peace. The terrors of God's law are effectually removed from us, and instead thereof we feel the drawings of his love. We are brought nigh by the atoning sacrifice, and have peace with God through Jesus Christ our Lord. We know that all his thoughts to us are thoughts of love, and we bless his name that our thoughts toward him are no longer those of the slave towards a taskmaster, or of a criminal towards a judge, but those of a beloved child towards a kind and tender father. Fervent love reigns in our hearts, casting out all fear and causing us to joy in God by our Lord Jesus Christ. This is a great blessing. It is surely a choice delight for a man to know that whether he prospers or is afflicted, whether he lives or dies, there is nothing between God and him but perfect amity; for all that offends has been effectually put away.

Beloved, when the apostle wishes us peace in the words of our text, he no doubt means that our hearts should be at perfect peace, by being placed fully in accord with the will of God; for, alas, we have known some, who we hope are forgiven and are God's children, who nevertheless quarrel with God very sadly. They are not pleased with what he does, but even complain that he deals hardly with them: they are naughty children, and carry on a sort of sullen contention with their heavenly Father, because he does not indulge them in all their whims and fancies. Now may the Lord of peace put an end to all such grievous warfare of heart in his people. May you love the Lord so well and trust him so fully that you could not pick a quarrel with him, even if he smote you and bruised you and broke your bones. Whatever he does is not only to be accepted with submission, but to be rejoiced in. That which pleases him should please us. Then have we perfect peace when we can magnify and praise the Lord even for the sharp cuts of his rod, and the fierce fires of his furnace. May the Lord bring us into this state, for there is no joy like it; perfect peace with God is heaven below.

Yea, brethren, we reach a little further than reconciliation and submission, for we come into the enjoyment of conscious complacency. There are men who are at peace with God as to the forgiveness of sin, and in a measure are in accord with his will, but they are not walking carefully in the path of obedience, and so they are missing the sense of divine love. God is their Father, and he loves them, but he hides his face from them; they walk contrary to him, and so he walks contrary to them. We cannot consider such a condition to be one of the fullest peace. The truly restful state of mind is enjoyed when the heart and life are daily cleansed by grace, so that there is nothing to grieve the Spirit of God, and therefore the Lord feels it right to favour his child with the light of his countenance in full meridian splendour. O how blessed to bask in the sunlight of Jehovah's love, free from all doubt, and having no more conscience of sin! In that sense of conscious favour lies the rest of heaven. May the Lord of peace himself give us this peace.

Peace because sin is forgiven, is the sweet fruit of justification—"therefore being justified by faith, we have peace with God." Peace because the heart is renewed and made to agree with the will of God is the blessed result of sanctification, for "to be spiritually minded is life and peace." Peace, because the soul is conscious of being the object of divine love, is a precious attendant upon the spirit of adoption, which is the very essence of peace. Brethren in Christ, may this threefold peace with God be with you always.

Now we look further and note that this peace spreads itself abroad and covers *all things* with its soft light. God is great, and filleth all things, and he who becomes at peace with him is at peace with all things else. Being reconciled to God, the believer says,—All things are mine, whether things present or things to come; all are mine, for I am Christ's and Christ is God's. Behold the Lord has made us to be in league with the stones of the field, and the beasts of the field are at peace with us. Providence is our pavilion, and angels are our attendants. All things work together for our good, now that we love God and are the called according to his purpose. No longer are we afraid for the terror by night, nor for the arrow that flieth by day, nor for the pestilence that walketh in darkness, nor for the destruction which wasteth at noonday. Behold the Lord God covereth us with his feathers, and under his wings do we trust; his truth is our shield and buckler: because we have set our love upon him he doth deliver us, and he doth set us on high because we have known his name. At peace with the Lord of hosts we are at peace with all the armies of the universe, in alliance with all the forces which muster at Jehovah's bidding. Though we must be at war with Satan, yet even he is chained and made as a slave to accomplish purposes of good contrary to his own will. There is neither in heaven nor earth nor hell anything that we need fear when we are once right with God. Settle the centre, and the circumference is secure: peace with God is universal peace.

This practically shows itself in the Christian's inward peace with regard to *his present circumstances*, be they what they may. Being at peace with God he sees the Lord's hand in everything around him, and is content. Is he poor? The Lord makes him rich in faith, and he asks not for gold. Is he sick? The Lord endows him with patience, and he glories in his afflictions. Is he laid aside from the holy service which he so much loves? He feels that the Lord knows best. If he might be actively engaged in doing God's will he would be very thankful, and run with diligence the race set before him; but if he must lie in the hospital, and suffer rather than serve, he does not wish to put his own wishes before the will of his Master, but he leaves himself in the Lord's hands, saying, "Lord, do as thou wilt with me. I am so at peace with thee that if thou use me I will bless thee, and if thou lay me aside I will bless thee: if thou spare my life I will bless thee, and if thou bring me down to the grave I will bless thee; if thou honour me among men I will bless thee, and if thou make me to be trodden under foot like straw for the dunghill I will still bless thee: for thou art everything, and I am nothing, thou art all goodness and I am sin and emptiness." The soul which thus has perfect peace as to all its personal surroundings is indeed happy; it is lying down in green pastures beside the still waters.

Blessed be God this peace is mainly to be found *in the soul itself* as to its own thoughts, believings, hopings, expectations, and desires. We have not only peace towards the outer world, but peace within. After all, happiness and peace lie more within the man than in anything about him. Heaven lies more in the heart than in golden streets, and hell's flame consists rather in man's tortured conscience than in the Tophet fire which the breath of God has kindled. So the peace which Jesus gives is within us; "the good man is satisfied from himself." Some minds are strangers to peace. How can they have peace, for they have no faith? They are as a rolling thing before the whirlwind, having no fixed basis, no abiding foundation of belief. These are the darlings of the school of modern thought, whose disciples set themselves as industriously to breed doubt as if salvation came by it. Doubt and be saved is their gospel, and who does not see that this is not the gospel of peace? Forsooth they are receptive, and are peering about for fresh light, though long ago the Sun of Righteousness has arisen. Such uncertainty suits me not. I must *know* something or I cannot live: I must be sure of something or I have no motive from which to act. God never meant us to live in perpetual questioning. His revelation is not and cannot be that shapeless cloud which philosophical divines make it out to be. There must be something true, and Christ must have come into the world to teach us something saving and reliable; he cannot mean that we should be always rushing through bogs and into morasses after the will-of-the-wisp of intellectual religion. There is assuredly some ascertainable, infallible, revealed truth for common people; there must be something sure to rest upon. I know that it is so, and declare unto you what I have heard and seen. There are great truths which the Lord has engraven upon my very soul, concerning which all the men on earth and all the devils in hell cannot shake me. As to these vital doctrines, an immovable and unconquerable dogmatism has laid hold upon my soul, and therefore my mind has peace. A man's mind must come to a settlement upon eternal truths by the teaching of the Holy Ghost, or else he cannot know what peace is.

I would ask for every one of my brethren that they may find an anchorage of mind and heart and never leave it. We have been often spoken of as an old-fashioned church, and your minister is said to be *Ultimus Puritanorum*, the last of the Puritans, a man incapable of any thought beyond the limit of the old-fashioned theology. I bless the Lord that it is even so. I am indeed incapable of forsaking the gospel for these new-fangled theories. Down went my anchor years ago: it was a great relief to me when I first felt it grip, and it is a growing joy to me that I know whom I have believed, and am persuaded that he is able to keep that which I have committed to him. Pretensions to original thought I have never made. I invent nothing, I only tell the old, old story as God enables me. "Ah," said a certain divine to me one day, "it must be very easy to you to preach because you know what you are going to say; your views are fixed and stereotyped. As for me," he said, "I am always seeking after truth, and I do not know one week what I may preach the next." Thus speak the teachers—do you wonder if the disciples wander into scepticism? Has the Lord taught the man nothing of sure truth? Then let him wait till he has received his message. Till he knows the gospel in his own heart experimentally as the power of God unto salvation let him sit on the penitent form and ask to be prayed for, but never enter a pulpit. What are the churches at to tolerate these sowers of infidelity? Time was when the fathers in our Israel would have chased from their pulpits those who glory in the unbelief which is their shame. May the Lord of peace himself give you peace as to your personal beliefs and convictions, and then when you get into deep waters of trial and sorrow you will say, "Ah, I did believe the right doctrine after all. I can feel the grip of my anchor on the things unseen. I have not been deceived. I have not followed cunningly devised fables, for the promise is true and I feel the power of it, it sustains and cheers and comforts me under all my trials, and I know that it will do so even to my dying hour." May every troubled thinker find the peace of faith and never lose it.

Many minds are for ever restless as to their fears. It is a great thing to know what you tremble at, for when you know what you fear your fear is half gone. The indefinable shape, the mysterious hand which has no arm, but writes upon the wall in strange characters,—the cloudiness of all things dreaded makes the mind more restless. But blessed is the man to whom the Lord has taught his fear, so that he knows what he fears, and does not permit his hopes to be in perpetual eclipse.

Of this many-sided peace we must say something more. The Thessalonian church had been troubled three ways. They had been *persecuted from without*. That is not a pleasant thing, but the apostle says, "You that are troubled rest with us." Now, when the Lord Jesus Christ says to a persecuted saint, "I am with you: all the evil which is done unto you is done unto me, and you are bearing it for my name's sake," then, beloved, no persecution can break the peace of the soul, but rather the sufferer rejoices and is exceeding glad that he is counted worthy, not only to believe in Christ, but to suffer for his sake.

Next, the Thessalonian church was annoyed by certain *false teachers*. They did not absolutely teach novel doctrine, but upon a basis of truth they erected an edifice of error. They exaggerated one special truth, and carried its teaching to extravagance. They said, Christ is coming, therefore the day of the Lord is immediately at hand. They belonged to that order of fanatics who are always raving about "the signs of the times," and pretending to know what will happen within the next twenty years. There were impostors of that sort in Paul's day, and there are such impostors now. Believe them not, they can see no more of the future than blind horses. I put them all together as impostors, whether they are preachers or literary hacks, for no man knoweth the future, and no man can tell his fellow about it. I care no more for their explanations of prophecy than for the pretended winking of the eyes of the Madonna; yet will they continue the cheat, and will be saying, one this thing, and another that, that this and that wonder shall happen, and that terrible judgments shall overwhelm our nation. The apostle would not have the Thessalonians disturbed in their minds by fears about the future. Brethren in Christ, the most terrible fact of the future can be no just cause of alarm to a true believer. The Lord comforts his people, and there is nothing in his plans or purposes which is intended to disquiet them. You may rest assured that if any doctrine in the Bible prevents a godly man from enjoying peace it must be because he has not yet understood it fully, or else has mistaken its bearing towards himself. Truth must minister peace to true men. All truth, whether doctrinal or prophetic, is on the side of the children of God; how can it be otherwise? The apostle tells the Thessalonians not to be disturbed about the coming of Christ. "The Lord be with you all," saith he, and if the Lord be with us, what matters it to us whether he personally comes at once or chooses to delay? We should be looking for his coming, but not with alarm, for the fact that he has come already is a well-spring of delight. We glory in his first advent, and do not dread the second: since we are already raised up into the heavenly places to sit with him by faith, what matters it to us whether he is up there or down here, or whether we are in heaven or on earth, so long as we abide in him. There may arise, possibly there will arise, wild fanatics who will again spread alarming news about wars and rumours of wars, and select some fatal year as the end of all things. Well, if such things should be, if crowds should go into the wilderness or into the city to look for the coming of Christ, believe them not, but sit ye still in peace and tranquillity of spirit and say, "My soul loves him and he loves me. He cannot mean ill to me whether he destroys the earth or spares it. Though the heavens pass away and the earth itself melt with fervent heat, my heart is resting in her Lord and knows herself to be secure." Thus the Lord saves his people from the disturbance caused by false teaching.

There were also in the church disorderly characters, people that went about spreading idle tales and gossiping.

They would not do anything for a living, and so they set people by the ears. But when the Lord gives a Christian man deep spiritual peace within, he soon puts aside the small nuisances of idle tongues and disorderly deeds. He refuses to be worried. Mosquitoes buzz around every Christian church, and blessed is the man who does not feel their bite or heed their buzzing; his soul shall dwell at ease. Peace from church troublers is a great blessing, and we ought to praise God for it when we are in the enjoyment of it, for strife within the church, like civil war, is the worst of warfare. O to live in holy love and unbroken concord in reference to all our fellow Christians. May the Lord of peace grant us this.

Thus, you see, the peace which is here spoken of has many sides to it. May you possess it in all its forms, modes, and phases, and may your spirit enter into the peace of God which passeth all understanding.

## II. Now, secondly, let us note the special desirableness of peace.

It is a very great thing for a soul to realize perfect peace, for if it does not do so, it must miss the joy, and comfort, and blessedness of the Christian life. God never meant his children to be like thistledown, wafted about with every breath, nor as a football, hurled to and fro by every foot. He meant us to be a happy, restful, established people. The cattle crop the grass, but they are not fattened till they lie down and ruminate in peace: the Lord makes his people to feed and to lie down in quietness. You do not know the gospel, dear friends, if you have not obtained peace through it; peace is the juice, the essence, the soul of the gospel. Doctrines are clusters, but you have never trodden them in the wine vat, you have never quaffed the flowing juice of their grapes if you have not peacefully considered divine truth in the quiet of your heart.

Without peace you cannot grew. A shepherd may find

good pasture for his flock, but if his sheep are hunted about by wild dogs, so that they cannot rest, they will become mere skin and bone. The Lord's lambs cannot grow if they are worried and harried; they must enjoy the rest wherewith the Lord maketh the weary to rest. If your soul is always sighing, and moaning, and questioning its interest in Christ, if you are always in suspense as to what doctrine is true and what is false, if there is nothing established and settled about you, you will never come to the fulness of the stature of a man in Christ Jesus.

Neither without peace can you bear much fruit, if any. If a tree is frequently transplanted you cannot reasonably look for many golden apples upon its boughs. The man who has no root-hold, who neither believes, nor grasps, nor enjoys the gospel, can never know what it is to be steadfast, unmovable, neither will he be always abounding in the work of the Lord.

We know, too, some who, because they have no conscious peace with God, lack all stability, and are the prey of error. That doctrine can soon be driven out of a man's head which affords no light and comfort to his heart. If you derive no sweetness from what you believe, I should not marvel if you soon begin to doubt it. The power of the gospel is its best evidence to the soul; a man always believes in that which he enjoys. Only make a truth to be a man's spiritual food, let it be marrow and fatness to him, and I warrant you he will believe it. When truth becomes to a proud carnal mind what the manna became to murmuring Israel, namely, light broad that his soul abhorreth, then the puffed up intellect cries after something more pleasing to the flesh; but to the mind which hungers and thirsts after righteousness the gospel is so soul-satisfying that it never wearies of it.

Brethren, you must have peace for your soul's wealth. What a difference there is between a soul at peace and a soul continually tossed about! I have seen one man's heart like a country whose hedges are broken down, whose walls are laid level with the ground, where irrigation is neglected, where tilling has ceased, where the vines are untrimmed, where the fields are unploughed, and all because there is a perpetual sound of war in the soul, and the song of peace is never heard. Such a soul may be likened to the Holy Land beneath Turkish rule, where no man has rest, and consequently the highways lie waste, and the gardens are a desert. But I have seen another man's life which has grown up under the influence of holy peace, from whom God has kept back the wandering Arabs of doubt and fear, and to whom he has given a settled government of grace and an establishment in steadfastness and quiet assurance, and, lo, that man has been as the land which floweth with milk and honey. As war spends and peace gathers the riches of nations, so does inward strife devour us, while spiritual peace makes the soul fat. Even as Palestine when it abounded in corn and wine and oil could nourish Tyre and Sidon, which border thereon, even so does the man who is rich towards God through internal peace become a feeder of other souls, till even they who are but borderers upon Immanuel's land obtain a blessing. Beloved, I would that every Christian knew this soul-enriching peace to the full. I am sorry to meet with so many who "hope" they are believers, and "trust" they are saved, but they are not sure. Ah, brethren, in these matters we must get beyond mere hopes, we must reach to certainties. "Ifs" and "buts" are terrible in the things which concern the soul and eternity. We must have plain and unquestionable security here, divine security applied to the soul itself by the Holy Ghost. Friend, you are either saved this morning or you are not saved; either you are in the love of God, or you are not; either you are secure of heaven, or you are not—one of the two. I beseech you, do not let these things be in jeopardy; chance anything rather than your soul. Cry mightily to God that you may have these things fixed, certain, positive, beyond all dispute, for then shall your soul enjoy peace with God, and so shall you become strong, useful, and happy.

**III. Now, thirdly, we shall get into the very heart of our text while we consider for a minute or two the sole person from whom this peace must come,—"Now the Lord of peace himself give you peace."**

Who is this "Lord of peace" but the Lord Jesus, the Prince of peace, born into the world when there was peace all over the world? It was but a little interval in which the gates of the temple of war were closed, and lo, Jesus came to Bethlehem, and angels sang, "Peace on earth." He came to establish an empire of peace which shall be universal, and under whose influence they shall hang the useless helmet high and study war no more. "The Prince of peace!" How blessed is the title! So was it written of old by Esaias, and Paul, the true successor of Isaiah, changing but a word, now speaks of "the Lord of peace." This is he who, being in himself essential peace, undertook to be the Father's great Ambassador, and having made peace by the blood of his cross, ended the strife between man and his offended Maker. This is he who is our peace, who hath made Jew and Gentile one, and broken down the middle wall of partition which stood between us. This is the Lord who, when he stood in the midst of his disciples, gave them peace by saying, "Peace be unto you"; and this is he who in his departure made his last will and testament, and wrote therein this grand legacy—"Peace I leave with you, my peace I give unto you; not as the world giveth give I unto you." This is that Lord of peace to whom it is part of his nature and office to give peace.

I want to call particular attention to the apostle's words in this place. He does not say "May the Lord of peace send his angel to give you peace." It were a great mercy if he did, and we might be as glad as Jacob was at Mahanaim, when the angels of God met him. He does not even say, "May the Lord of peace send his minister to give you peace." If he did we might be as happy as Abraham when Melchizedec refreshed him with bread and wine. He does not even say, "May the Lord of peace at the communion table, or in reading the word, or in prayer, or in some other sacred exercise give you peace." In all these we might well be as refreshed as Israel was at Elim where wells and palm trees gladdened the tribes; but he says "the Lord of peace *himself* give you peace," as if he alone in his own person could give peace, and as if his presence were the sole means of such a divine peace as he desires.

"The Lord of peace himself give you peace." The words are inexpressibly sweet to me. If you will think for a minute you will see that we never do obtain peace except from the Lord himself. What after all in your worst times will bring you peace? I will tell you. "This man shall be the peace." To me it has often afforded great peace to think of his mysterious person. He is a man tempted in all points like as I am, a man who knows every grief of the soul and every pain of the body, hence his tender sympathy and power to succour. Have you not often derived peace from that sweet reflection? You know you have. His person then is a source of peace. And have you not been rested in your soul by meditating upon his death? You have viewed him wounded, bleeding, dying on the tree; and, insensibly to yourself, a wondrous calm has stolen over your heart, and you have felt pacified concerning all things. Yes, Jesus is himself that bundle of myrrh and spice from which peace flows like a sweet perfume. When he comes very near your heart and lays bare his wounds, and speaks his love home to you, making you feel its divine fervency, when he assures you that you are one with him, united to him in an everlasting wedlock, which knows of no divorce—then it is that your soul is steeped in peace. This is an experimental business and no mere words can express it. "The Lord of peace himself give you peace,"— this, I say, he does mainly by manifesting himself to the heart of his servants.

Then notice that the text says, "*give* you peace," not merely offer it to you, or argue with you that you ought to have peace, or show you the grounds of peace, but "give you peace." He has the power to breathe peace into the heart, to create peace in the soul, and lull the spirit into that sweet sleep of the beloved which is the peculiar gift of heaven. "I will give you rest," said he, and he can and will do it.

"*The Lord be with you all*": as much as to say, "That is what I mean." I pray that Jesus may be with you, for if he is present you must enjoy peace. Let the sea rage and let every timber of the ship be strained; yea, let her leak till between each timber there yawns a hungry mouth to swallow you up quick; yet when Jesus arises he will rebuke the winds and the waves, and there will be a great calm. "It is I, be not afraid," is enough to create peace at once. May you always know this peace which Jesus alone can give.

**IV. Now I must conclude with the fourth head, which is a consideration of the sweep of the prayer— "The Lord of peace himself give you peace *always*."**

What! *always* at peace? Yes, that is what the apostle desires for you. May you have peace given you *always*. "Well, sir, I feel very happy on Sabbath-days. I have such peace that I wish I could have a week of Sundays." May the Lord himself give you peace *always*, on all the week days as well as on the Lord's days. "Truly, I have been very happy of late," says one, "God has prospered us and everyone has been very loving in the family; but I do not know how I should be if I had an awkward husband and unruly children." Sister, I will tell you what I want you to be,—I would have you restful under all circumstances,— "The Lord of peace give you peace always." "I enjoy such peace in the prayer-meeting," says one. I want you to have peace in the workshop also. "I do have peace when I get alone with my Bible," cries another. We pray that you may have equal peace when you are troubled with the ledger, and tired with those unpaid bills, and dull trade, and cross currents of business. You need peace always. Our friends who are commonly called Quakers have, as a rule, set us a fine example of calm, dignified quietness and peace. How undisturbed they generally appear. Whatever they fail in they certainly excel in a certain peacefulness of manner which I hope is the index of calm enjoyed within. Numbers of professors are very fretful, excitable, agitated, hasty, and fickle. It should not be so, brethren; you ought to have more weight about you, more grace, more solidity. Your soul's affairs are all right, are they not? All is right for ever, everything is signed, sealed, and delivered; the covenant is ordered in all things and sure, and everything is in divine hands for our good. Well, then, why not let us be as happy as the angels are? Why are we troubled? Is there anything worth shedding a tear for now that all is well for eternity? Our want of peace arises from the fact that we have not realized the fulness of our text. "The Lord of peace himself give you peace always." He can always give you peace, for he never changes; there is always the same reason for peace; you may always go to him for peace, and he is always ready to bestow it. Oh that we might always possess it!

Notice, again, it is written—"May the Lord of peace give you peace always *by all means*." Can he give us peace by all means? I know he can give us peace by some means, but can all means be made subservient to this end? Some agencies evidently work towards peace, but can he give us peace by opposing forces? Yes, certainly: he can give peace by the bitter as well as by the sweet, peace by the storm as well as by the calm, peace by loss as well as by gain, peace by death as well as by life. For, notice there are two grand ways of giving us peace: and one is by taking away all that disquiets us. Here is a man who frets because he does not make money, or because he has lost much of his wealth. Suppose the Lord takes away from him all covetousness, all greed of gain, all love of the world—is he not at once filled with peace? He is at peace not because he has more money, but because he has less of grasping desire. Another man is very ambitious, he wants to be somebody, he must be great, and yet he never will be, and therefore he is restless. Suppose the grace of God should humble him and take away his lofty aspirations, so that he only wishes to be and to do what the Lord wills. Do you not see how readily he rests? Another man has an angry temper, and is soon put out: the Lord does not alter the people that are round about him, but he changes the man himself, makes him quiet, ready to forgive, and of a gentle spirit. What peace the man now feels! Another person has had an envious eye—he did not like to see others prosper, and if others were better off than himself he always thought hardly of them. The Lord wrings that bitter drop of envy out of his heart, and now see how peaceful he is—he is glad to see others advanced, and if he is tried himself it helps to make him happy to think that others are more favoured. It is a great blessing when the Lord removes the disturbing elements from the heart. Even curiosity may be a source of unrest. Many are a great deal worried by curiosity. I have sometimes wanted to know why the Lord does this and that with me. Blessed be his name, I am resolved not to question him any more in that fashion. Somebody prayed the other day that I might see the reason why the Lord has lately afflicted me. I hope the brother will not pray that any more, for I do not want to know the Lord's reasons—why should I? I know he has done right, and I will not dishonour him by catechising him and wanting him to explain himself to a poor worm. This is where the mischief has been with most of us, that we have wanted to see how this and that can be right. Why should we? If God conceals a thing let us be anxious to keep it concealed. A servant was passing through a street with a dish that was curiously covered. There met him a fellow who said, "I am most anxious to know what thy lord has put in that dish, for he has so carefully covered it." But the the servant said, "Therefore shouldst thou not desire to know, for seeing my lord has so carefully covered it, it is clear that it is no business of thine." So whenever a providence puzzles you take it as a sign that the Lord does not mean you to understand it, and be content to take it upon faith. When curiosity and other restless things are gone peace is enjoyed.

Then the Lord has ways of giving us peace by making discoveries of himself. Some of you do not know as yet the things which would give you peace. For instance, if you did but know that he loved you from before the foundation of the world, and that whom once he loves he never leaves, you who are now afraid that you have fallen from grace would obtain strong consolation. Ay, and if you understood the grand doctrine of the divine decree, and saw that the Lord will not fail nor be discouraged, nor turn aside from one jot or tittle of his purpose, then you would see how you, poor insignificant believers though you be, are one stitch in the great fabric that must not be suffered to drop, or else the whole fabric will be marred. You would understand how the eternal purpose ordered in wisdom, and backed up with sovereign power, guarantees your salvation as much as it does the glory of God, and so you would have peace.

Many a soul has not the peace it might have, because it does not fully understand the atoning blood. The great doctrine of substitution is not seen in all its length and breadth by some minds. But when they come to see Christ standing in the place of his chosen, made sin for them, and the chosen standing in Christ's place, "the righteousness of God in him," then will their peace be like a river. The grand truth of the union of the saints with Christ, if it be once understood, what a means of peace it is! He that believeth in Christ is one with him, a member of his body, of his flesh, and of his bones, one with Christ by eternal and indissoluble union, even as the Father is one with the

Son. If this be known, together with the doctrine of the covenant, the attribute of immutability, the eternal purpose, and the marriage union between Christ and his elect, deep peace must be enjoyed, like the calm of heaven, like the bliss of immortality.

But there are some to whom this peace cannot come, some concerning whom the Lord saith "What hast thou to do with peace?" "There is no peace, saith my God, unto the wicked." Your works, your prayers, your repentances, none of these can bring you peace. As for the world and the pleasures thereof, they are destructive to all hope of peace. Come ye this day and believe in the great sacrifice which God himself has prepared in the person of his crucified Son. Come look into Emanuel's face and read where peace is to be found. Come to the great gash in Jesus' side and see the cleft of the rock where God's elect abide in peace. Trust in Jesus and you shall begin a peace which shall widen and deepen into the peace of God which passeth all understanding, which shall keep your hearts and minds by Christ Jesus. Amen.

# 5
## SWEET PEACE FOR TRIED BELIEVERS

*"These things I have spoken unto you, that in me ye might
have peace. In the world ye shall have tribulation:
but be of good cheer; I have overcome the world."
—John 16:33.*

*"So let us consider that every battle-field to which God calls
us is only another opportunity of victory, and,
Christ being with us, another certainty of victory.
Onward, then, ye Christian soldiers!"*

~

This most delightful passage occurs at the close of the
last of our Saviour's sermons before he went unto the
Father. Let us treasure it as we lay up a man's last words.
Wonderfully full that sermon is: it is of a piece with his last
prayer, and that rises above all other pleadings of men.
This farewell discourse may occupy but a short space in
Scripture, but the thoughts suggested by it are so many
that I suppose that the world itself might hardly contain
the books that might fairly be written upon it. It took our
Lord but a moment to speak some of its sentences; it will
take us a lifetime fully to understand them. Peradventure
we never shall understand some of these gracious sayings

till we have put away all childish things, and shall have come to the fulness of the stature of men in Christ Jesus. We shall never see all the richness of the grace of this sermon till we have risen beyond these mists and clouds into the clearer atmosphere of the unclouded skies. In that happy country, being ourselves raised to a nobler condition, we shall be better able to comprehend the deep things of God, concerning which our Saviour spake in his supreme discourse. Meanwhile, let us apply our heart and mind to the consideration of these last words of the greatest of all preachers, the dearest of all teachers; and may the Spirit of our God open them up to us!

Observe concerning the preaching of our Lord Jesus how eminently practical it is. You never find in the Master's speaking a single sentence spoken for what orators use to call "effect." He never introduces a pretty bit here and there to let men see how poetical his mind could be. He never goes a little aside to introduce a something which was quite unnecessary to the display of the subject, but very necessary to the display of the orator. Nothing so little, so self-seeking, ever governs the mind of Jesus. Far from it. His soul goes with his subject, and he has no second object: he would convey his meaning to his hearers, and his mind is concentrated on that aim. He keeps hard at it, steadily driving at his point, and he speaks ever with the one desire, that the truth should go home to the heart, and should be blessed to the hearer. Hence he adopted the method in this instance of summing-up, and doing what the old divines used to call "making the improvement" at the end, when the truth which they had spoken was turned to practical account, and the uses of the topic were enlarged upon. We might have found out, perhaps, by diligent study, what the practical drift of the Saviour's discourse was; for it is never difficult for a spiritual mind to perceive his drift; but he meant not only that we might possibly see what he was aiming at, but that we should be sure of seeing it; and so he puts it into the plainest language, and he says, "These things have I spoken unto you, that in me ye might have peace."

If this was our Lord's object, I do not doubt that he had fully accomplished it. All that he had said tended to produce peace in his disciples' hearts; but he knew that their minds were dark—that they had but slight capacity as yet, and so in his infinite tenderness he told them, as one might tell a child, what he intended his address to produce. We thank him for this, and herein would we endeavour to copy him. We hope that our friends will always bear with us when we try to be very plain and simple, and spend much of our strength in pointing out what is the practical bearing of the truth which we are teaching. It will be better to be considered needlessly explicit than to miss the end we have in view.

Let us greatly prize this conclusion of the Saviour's ministry. It is all the more endeared to some of us by the fact that *our Lord finished as he began*. He is our peace; he came to bring it, and he left it behind him as he went away. Even before he had commenced his life-work it was announced of him that he came to bring "peace on earth, good will toward men"; and ere he is taken up, his last words must needs be "Peace I leave with you, my peace I give unto you." It was meet that he should close the service of his life wherein he had preached peace, by pronouncing this as his dismissary benediction. "These things have I spoken unto you, that in me ye might have peace."

In trying to handle this text to-night, aiming at the same practical end as my divine Lord and Master, I shall notice, first of all, *the believer in Christ*, and in Christ he is at peace; secondly, *the believer in the world*, and in the world he has tribulation; and, thirdly, *the believer in the world and in Christ*, and in that condition he has victory. "Be of good cheer; I have overcome the world." May the Holy Spirit, the Lord and giver of peace, bless the word which I may now speak unto you!

## I. First, you have the believer in Christ spoken of in reference to his peace.

Jesus saith—"That in me ye might have peace." It is worthy of careful consideration that in Jesus himself there was ever present an abiding peace. *He had peace.* If he had not himself possessed peace, we could not have had peace in him. But what a holy calm there was upon the spirit of our divine Master! Read his life through, and dwell upon any one delightful characteristic, and you will find him perfect; but if you study it carefully in order to remark upon his manliness, his self-possession, his calm and peaceful bearing in the midst of turmoil and provocation, you will find him to be a master of the art of peace. Truly in patience he possessed his soul. Never man had more to disturb him, but never man was less disturbed. He could not be turned aside from anything which he had resolved to do, for he set his face like a flint; and in the doing of it he could not be excited or discouraged, for his spirit was not of this changing world. Men might oppose him, but he endured great contradiction of sinners against himself with marvellous longsuffering. When his eager and foolish disciples would push him forward, or would hold him back, he was moved neither in the one direction nor in the other by any of them; but he steadfastly held to the even tenor of his way, his soul abiding in God, giving glory to God, and resting in the eternal Power and Godhead which he knew to be always at his side. The background of the life of Christ is the omnipresence of the Father. Wherever you see him—if you see him quite alone when every disciple has forsaken him—you see this text expounded, "Ye shall leave me alone, and yet I am not alone, because the Father is with me."

Now this fact that he felt the presence of the Father, and did not occasionally speak to God, but *dwelt* with him—that he did not resort to God as a make-shift in time of trouble, but abode with God at all times, and so kept his spirit above everything that would draw it down; this it was that filled him with an unbroken peace. Even Gethsemane did not break that peace. Covered with the bloody sweat he still cries, "Not as I will, but as thou wilt." When his soul is exceeding sorrowful, even unto death, yet he knows where his Father is, and he keeps his hold upon him, and maintains his intimacy with him. He feels that one word from him would presently bring more than twelve legions of angels to his rescue. Such is the position of favour which he still occupies with God, even when the sin of man is laid upon him. O friends, Christ has peace enough and to spare. He is himself, personally, the deep well-spring of an endless peace, and therefore we can understand why we always find peace in him. One calm and quiet man has sometimes spread peace through what else would have been terrified company. One Paul standing in the sinking ship saves all from ruin by the majesty of his immovable courage; and one Christ—such a Christ as ours—in the midst of a church turns a horde of cowards into an army of heroes. His infinite peace breathes peace into our vacillating spirits. We rest because we see how he rests.

Now, as the Master had peace in himself, *he had a strong desire that all his disciples should have peace.* I was about to say that it was with our Lord "the ruling passion strong in death." It was strong within him when he was coming very near his passion, and was about to go into Gethsemane, and then to Golgotha. Quietly he said, "These things have I spoken unto you, that in me ye might have peace." Our Lord Jesus Christ delights to see his people firm, calm, happy. I do not think that he is so pleased to see them excited, although we have those around us who seem to think that great grace can only display itself by raving and raging. The religion of the quiet Jesus was never intended to drive us to the verge of insanity. "He shall not strive, nor cry; neither shall any man hear his voice in the streets."

His Holy Spirit is no raven or eagle, but a dove: his holy influences are powerful, and therefore calm. Weakness hurries, rages, shouts; for it has need to do so. Strength moves with its own deliberate serenity, and effects its purpose. To those who think that saints should be maniacs, Jesus says, "Peace! Peace!"

On the other hand we are quite certain that our Lord Jesus does not desire his disciples to be depressed. To some the fit colour for piety seems to be grey, drab, or full mourning. But it is not so: the saints are arrayed in white linen, which is the emblem of gladness as well as of purity. The Saviour does not wish his disciples to go through the world as through a twilight of sadness, whispering in fear, because of judgments to come, and suppressing all joy because of the evils with which they are surrounded. No, brethren, Jesus wishes us all to be happy in himself, with a quiet peacefulness like his own. He was no laughing maker of merriment, but still he was serenely confident, and he would have us keep to his pitch, and be at peace. "These things have I spoken unto you, that in me ye might have peace."

We have a great end to serve; we have a grand life to live; we have a grand Helper ready to help us if we will but believe in him; therefore, we need not blow a trumpet before we begin, and we need not make a fuss when we are in the midst of our service, nor need we lie down on the ground as if we were the most wretched of men because of our heavenly calling. No, but we may just feel, "The Lord of hosts is with us; the God of Jacob is our refuge," and walk with God through life in that holy quiet which springs of conscious strength. Let us enjoy the calm of heart which comes of knowing that the reserves of God are infinite, and that at any moment they can come to the front and deliver us should an emergency occur. Oh, that we could learn from Christ the art of peace! He desires that we should have it. Then we should not be so often up and so speedily down, to-day so brimming over and to-morrow so empty, one moment so fast and another so slow, unduly exhilarated at one moment and at the next so needlessly depressed. We ought not to be movable as waves, but fixed as stars. We ought not to be as thistle-down, the sport of every wind, but as yonder granite peak, which defies the storms of the ages. "These things have I spoken unto you, that in me ye might have peace"—"peace." Oh, to get it, and to keep it, through Jesus Christ our Lord!

Thus I have noticed that he had peace, and he wished us to have it.

But now notice again that *in order to their having peace he spoke to them certain words*—"These things have I spoken to you, that in me ye might have peace." It will do you good, when you are at home, to read over the preceding chapter, and note with diligence what the Lord Jesus said in order to give his disciples peace, for that same thing will give *us* peace. If you please you may go back to the fifteenth chapter, and even to the fourteenth, where you read—"Let not your heart be troubled." When you are at it, you may, if you like, go all through the Book, backward or forward, searching for peace as for a pearl, and you will not err even then; for the great object of all these Scriptures which in the deepest sense were all spoken by Jesus Christ is that you may have peace. But especially let us dwell upon these particular words in this sixteenth chapter of John, for to these he chiefly alludes.

Now, what did he say to them that they might have peace? One thing was that *he foretold their trials*. He said to them, "They shall put you out of the synagogues: yea, the time cometh, that whosoever killeth you will think that he doeth God service." Learn then that one way for you to gain peace is to reflect upon it that trial is promised you, that trial is in the covenant, that persecution and the ill-will of an ungodly world are evils which you are bound to endure. They are guaranteed to you by the very fact of your being of the seed of the woman whose heel must be bruised; and they will come to you in your measure. Expect trials as you look for clouds and rain in the English climate. If this island be your dwelling-place, you cannot look for the climate of India; neither ought you to complain of winter and frost, for these are a part of a Briton's inheritance. You must take the rough with the smooth. When exceedingly severe persecutions and afflictions happen to you, they will seem to the adversary to be evident tokens of perdition; but to you they will be evident tokens of the truth of God's word, and of your being yourself a true lineal descendant of that persecuted Saviour who told you, "If they persecute me, they will also persecute you. The disciple is not above his Master, nor the servant above his Lord." Do, then, make yourself familiar with trial. Wonder when it does *not* come; and when it does come, say, "Ah! you are an old acquaintance of mine." There is such a thing as carrying the cross till you are so accustomed to it that you would be almost uneasy without it. You may bear a burden on your back so long that, if that burden were taken away, you would feel the miss of it. The Lord has made some of his children fond of the cross. It was so with Rutherford. He said at last that he was half afraid lest the cross, which had become so sweet to him, might rival Christ himself. I never feel any fear of *that* myself, for pain is very much dreaded by my coward flesh; but I suppose that there are saints who have come to feel that the bitter is so beneficial, that they would prefer its tonic to the sweetest cup that was ever mingled. It is an acquired taste, no doubt, but he that hath it will be at peace about trouble. It shall help you greatly to attain peace if you expect rough treatment while you are a sojourner in this present evil world.

The next thing he did to comfort them was, that *he told them why he was going away.* It is often a choice blessing, when you have a great trial, to know what it is sent for. That is a wise petition if not pressed too far—"Show me wherefore thou contendest with me." The Saviour was going, because it was expedient for them that he should go. Does it not take away the sting of a trial when you know by faith that it is expedient that such and such a grief should happen to you? If it is expedient that the dear child should be taken from your arms—expedient that the business should not prosper—expedient that you yourself should be struck with a sickness which no faith will remove, then you bow to the divine wisdom. The God who is better to you than all your fears, yea, better than your hopes, perhaps intends the affliction to remain with you until it lifts the latch of heaven for you, and lets you into your eternal rest. Now, when the Saviour told them why he was going, the condescending information was meant to produce peace in their hearts. He has also told you why your trials are sent to you: they work your lasting good: wherefore rest concerning them.

Further, to give them peace, the Saviour went on *to speak to them of the Holy Ghost, the Comforter, and what the Comforter would do*. He enlarged upon that theme, since it was so cheering. Beloved, if you want peace think much of the divine Comforter. You are not left alone. You are not left without the tenderest sympathy of One who knows how to cheer the heaviest heart. You are not left without a friend more able than all other friends to enter into your secret griefs, and administer to you the most potent consolations. Think much of the Holy Ghost in his office as Comforter, and the meditation will foster peace within your spirit. How ill we treat the Holy Spirit by our few and superficial thoughts of him! Let us henceforth adore him with deeper love and reverence.

Then he told them about *the power of prayer*. He said, "Whatsoever ye shall ask the Father in my name, he will give it you"; and again "If ye abide in me, and my words abide in you, ye shall ask what ye will, and it shall be done unto you." What a breath of peace cools the forehead of the man who remembers that he may pray, and that prayer is heard in heaven! There is a noise in the streets, there is a disturbance within doors, even your own heart is perturbed; what then? Let us pray. The known remedy for unknown evils is prayer. Oh, the peace that comes from the mercy-seat! You that are familiar with it will bear me witness that it is wonderful what storms it will quell, what cyclones it will quiet. Only pray, and thou art master of the situation. Like thy Master, thou mayest walk the waves of the sea, when thou hast but the power in his name to speak to those waves, and bid them be still; and he gives thee that power when thou drawest near to him in believing prayer.

All this must have greatly tended to produce peace; but as if this might not be enough, our tender Lord let slip a precious word that ought to give peace to all our minds: "*The Father himself loveth you.*" The love of God the Father is a treasure-house of peace. The *Father himself*—not moved by the importunities of his pleading Son, but himself, of his own accord, loveth you. O Father God, how hast thou sometimes been slandered, as though thou wert backward to love us, and thy Son must needs persuade thee! Nay, it is not so. God loved his people, and, therefore he sent his Son to redeem them. "He so loved the world that he gave his only begotten Son." Christ is not the cause of divine love, but the sweetest and best fruit of it. "The Father himself loveth you." Wherefore, be of good cheer, and let your peace be like a river.

And then, dear friends, *he confirmed their faith in himself.* He so spoke to them that at last they said, "Now are we sure. By this we believe," and so on. This is the way to get peace. Peace comes by the way of faith. Those of you who are very fond of doubts, can, perhaps, tell me whether you ever derived any peace from them. Time is but ill-used when we pore over books which are calculated to shake our faith: as well eat food which is sure to make us ill. There are certain men who are always busy with the Scriptures to try and find difficulties in them; and if they cannot find them in the English version, then straightway they will sooner have a new translation than miss their precious difficulty. This is as foolish as if we should refuse to eat our Christmas pudding because we could not find any stones in the plums, or any hard lumps in the sugar to break our teeth upon. The great object of some men seems to be to find in the Bible something which they cannot believe: for my part I am delighted with what I do believe. They cultivate doubts, while a wise man regards them as weeds, and burns them in a heap. The Lord knows there is sorrow enough in this world without labouring to make more; and I should like to ask all such critics and great discoverers whether they believe that their discoveries tend at all to the creation of peace in their own minds, or in the minds of others? I believe, and then I get peace. I believe and am sure: then is my peace like a river, and my righteousness like the waves of the sea. Luther tells us how he found peace when one said to him, "I believe in the forgiveness of sins." Oh, if one did but believe what he professes to believe! I mean believed it fully! That way lies peace—in believing up to the hilt. The child-like way of sitting at Jesus' feet, and receiving his words—this is the path of peace. All the outgrowth of quibbling and cavilling may be summed up as thorns and briers, tearing the flesh and rending the spirit. These things had Christ spoken, that they might believe in him, for well he knew that the victory which overcomes trial is faith, and not doubt. Believing, and not questioning, is the King's highway.

I must notice that *our Master's wish that we might have peace was qualified by those two words, "in me"*—"That *in me* ye might have peace." Remember, then, you may not expect to derive peace from yourselves. You will turn that dunghill over a long while before you find the jewel of peace in it. Our Lord did not even intend that we should find peace in outward ordinances, or religious exercises. No doubt it is very quieting to read a chapter, or to attend a service, or to come to communion; but it is not the Lord's intent that these should of themselves yield us peace. These are to be means to peace, but the peace must always be *in himself*, in his own blessed Person. We must get to him, for this is his wish, "that *in me* ye might have peace"—peace only in him, but peace always in him. Peace of the deepest, truest, most constant, most emphatic kind is only found in Jesus. Peace in all seasons, and in all difficulties; peace for ever: all this is in him, and in him only. Outside of him it is all tossing to and fro, and question, and fog, and haze, and fear; but in him we dwell as in a sheep-fold, where the sheep lie down and rest. In him we are in a home where all is love and comfort. Brothers, sisters, let us not wander from this sacred centre of serene repose, lest we wander from peace. It is this man who shall be the peace, this Son of God who shall give us rest; let us then come to him at once in every case; yea, let us evermore abide in him. His wish is that his joy may be in us, and therefore he says, "These things have I spoken unto you, that in me ye might have peace."

Thus have I said well-nigh enough to you upon this first point of the believer in Christ, and his peace.

**II. I have been a long while on that head, and I want to be all the shorter on the second—the believer in the world finds himself like wheat under the flail, for so the text puts it, "In the world ye shall have tribulation."**

That is, first, *you are not screened from any kind of trouble.* You are in Christ, and the Saviour saves you from your sins, but he has not promised that you shall have no sorrow. He has not promised to screen you from either poverty, or toil, or sickness, or slander, or any of the common ills of mankind. Some of the very best of his beloved have been enriched and indulged by being permitted to undergo much secret discipline of pain, and sorrow, and want. Your Lord, among the treasures that he gives you, grants a cross. You start back, and say, "Not *that*, Lord;" but he answers, "Yes, *this*, my child. This and no other." The cross is the best piece of furniture in your house, though you have sometimes wished it was not there. It shall always work your good: it does work it now. Some of the comforts allotted to you in providence will be questionable in their effect upon you, by reason of your sinfulness and weakness; but the cross which the Lord appoints you has no result but your good. It is a bitter tree, apparently, but it is a healthful medicine. Take it, child of God; plant it, and let it grow, and its fruit shall be sweet." We are not guarded from tribulation, but we are promised it, and we are benefited by it.

*We are not favoured by being promised the admiration of the ungodly.* "In the world"—not merely in this present state, but in this ungodly world—we shall have tribulation. Worldlings will not gather round you to admire your excellence and assist your piety. If they did I should think that either the world had changed, or else it had made a mistake about you. Which of the two it is I do not say. I do not think that it can be that the world has changed. Worldlings may like a Christian for certain externals; they may admire him for certain advantages they get from him; but as a Christian they cannot love him. That is impossible. There is an enmity between the seed of the serpent and the seed of the woman; and you had better understand that it is so, because the serpent has not changed his nature, but is a vile deceiver and destroyer still. He still exhibits his glittering scales, and speaks as craftily and flatteringly to us as he did to mother Eve; and, perhaps, to you he says that he loves you more than he can tell, only you are so unfriendly and suspicious that he has never been able to show his affection. Yes, he sees in you so much to admire that he wishes you were not quite so strait-laced, and then he could introduce you to his dear friends and children, for you would do them no end of good. Hit him across the head if you get an opportunity, for he means no good to you. Of all the devils in the world I hate a roaring devil least; but a fawning devil is the worst devil that ever a man meets. When the world pretends to love, understand that it now hates you more cordially than ever, and is carefully baiting its trap to catch you and ruin you. Beware of the Judas kiss with which the Christ was betrayed, and with which you will be betrayed unless you are well upon your guard. In the world and from the world ye shall have tribulation.

The text puts this in such a broad way that it gives a hint that in the world you will have tribulation *often*. Affliction is not with us always, but it is well to be always prepared for it. There are times in which we enjoy prosperity: some Christians enjoy much of it; and do not let them be much alarmed because they do so, for what the Lord's providence sends us is not harmful in itself, and is to be accepted without suspicion. I remember that a person came to me once, and told me that she had prayed for affliction. I replied, "Dear soul, dear soul, do not be so foolish. You will have quite enough trouble without asking for it." If a child were to ask his father to let him be birched, he would be a strange sort of child, and I should think he would not be likely to repeat the experiment if he had a practical man for a father. No, no, no! That is not our path of duty. If God spares us tribulation let us be thankful to him; but if he does not spare us let us be equally thankful. This last is a hard lesson to learn; but we ought to learn it. We shall frequently endure tribulation, for we are born to it at our first birth, as the sparks fly upward. It is also certain that our second birth introduces us to a second set of tribulations. He sang a true song who gave us this verse,—

" 'Poor and afflicted,' 'tis their lot,

They know it, and they murmur not;

'Twould ill become them to refuse

The state their Master deign'd to choose."

Again, in the world ye shall *emphatically* have tribulation. If anybody else has it you shall; and if nobody else has it, yet you shall have it. You shall have it, perhaps, where you least wish it or reckon on it. "A man's foes shall be they of his own household." "Any cross but the one I have," cried one. Surely it would not be a cross if you had the choosing of it, for it is of the essence of a cross that it should run counter to our likings. It must be something from which the flesh shrinks, which is not for the present joyous but grievous. So our Lord puts it, "In the world ye shall have tribulation." I wonder how many Christians here could say that they have *not* found it so. I think that the most of us—at least, all I know of—would say that the prophecy of our Lord has been abundantly verified. And must it not be so in the nature of things? Has not this world been a place of sorrow ever since Adam broke his Maker's command? Did not the mandate then go forth, "Thorns also and thistles shall it bring forth to thee. Dust thou art, and unto dust shalt thou return"? To a Christian man must not the world bring tribulation and anguish because it is a world which lieth in the wicked one. The Christian is not of the world, even as Christ is not of the world. He is out of his element. He is an alien. He is a pilgrim. Can he expect the comforts of home while he tarries here? It is a world uncongenial to his spiritual nature. There is nothing in it to help him. This world is a foe to grace, and not a friend to it; and hence the gracious man must have tribulation. If he is to be like his Lord he certainly will have it; and if he is to be like the Lord's people, he will have it, for they are a line of cross-bearers. There is no exception to this rule if you take the whole of any believer's life, though for a while certain favoured men may seem to be the darlings of providence. Job multiplied his riches, and dwelt at ease with a hedge about him. He thought, perhaps, that he would have no tribulation to bear; but the flail seemed made of iron when at last it fell. So may the most prosperous have all the greater trial when the day of adversity arrives.

Brethren, I was thinking, as I turned over this subject, that though there is tribulation in the world, we still get far too fond of the world. We are always trying to pluck handfuls of its flowers; and if its roses had no thorns we should bury ourselves in heaps of them! We should never quit the nest and learn to fly if the Lord did not stir up our nest even as doth the eagle. We should want to tarry here for ever, and say, "Lo, this is my home," if it were not that an unkind world gives us aliens' treatment, and forces us to feel that here we are in exile. One said to a great man, as he looked over his gardens, "These are the things that make it hard to die." As we are not to live here, but must soon be up and away to the better land where our life can far better develop, it is meet that in the world we should have tribulation, that we may turn our thoughts and our desires towards that dear city of our God where alone is our dwelling place. Thanks be unto God for the tribulation which weans our thoughts from earth, and wins them for heaven; and let all the people say, "Amen."

**III. But now, lastly, let us view the believer in the world and in Christ; and this means victory. I will occupy but a moment or two to say, that if we dwell in Christ, though we have also to dwell in the world, yet we shall overcome the World.**

I call your special attention to the words of our Lord Jesus in the text—"Be of good cheer; I have overcome the world." *Our Lord was at that time still in the world.* Do you know where Christ was when he said *that?* Why, he was on the edge of Gethsemane. He was at the foot, so to speak, of Golgotha, where he was to die. He had not then borne the scourge and the cross. But I dare not lay my hand upon my Master, and say, "Good Lord, thou hast made a mistake. Thou hast not yet overcome, for the worst part of the battle has not come to thee." He knew what he said, and made no error in saying it. Oh, but it was bravely spoken! The faith which abode in him made him say, "I have overcome." On the verge of the fight he said, "I have overcome." John caught up this word when he afterwards said, "This is the victory which overcometh the world, even our faith," because it was by faith that our blessed Lord said at this moment, "I have overcome the world." He spoke in the prescience of faith. He took for granted that he would overcome the world, for the Father was with him.

But up to that point it was assuredly true, as it was even to the end, that *he had really overcome the world*. Its blandishments he had overcome. Its temptations he had overcome. Its terrors he had overcome. Its errors he had overcome. Everything in the world that had assailed him he had put to the rout. He was tempted in all points like as we are; but he remained without sin. He had overcome everything that had come to attack his holiness, his patience, his self-sacrifice: he had been victor at every point.

Now, here is a matter of joyful consideration: our Lord says, "Be of good cheer; I have overcome the world." But what cheer is there in that? Well, the cheer lies in the fact which he does not here state, but which he had stated before, namely, that *he is one with us, and we are one with him.* He does as good as say, "I have overcome the world, and you are in me, your Head. My overcoming of the world belongs to you. I, your Leader, have overcome the world for you. I have led the way in this dread fight, and conquered the adversaries which you have now to fight with, and thus I have virtually won the battle before you begin it."

"Hell and thy sins obstruct thy course,
But hell and sins are vanquished foes:
Thy Jesus nailed them to his cross,
And sang the triumph when he rose."

"I have myself," says Jesus, "overcome for you that you may overcome in me. Now, go you to the fight, to rout the already worsted enemy, and triumph over a serpent whose head I have already broken."

*We derive, then, from the fact that Christ has overcome, the assurance that we shall overcome*, since we are one with him, members of his body, and parts of himself. O brothers, sisters, you must fight your way through. You cannot quit this conflict. You have to cut your way through a solid wall of difficulties: there is no other course! But you are going to do it. You shall do it. A great commander commences a campaign. Does he desire that there shall be no battle? If so, how is it a war? How is he a soldier? He certainly can send home no reports of victory if there is no fighting. He can never come to be a great commander if he never distinguishes himself in the field. So let us consider that every battle-field to which God calls us is only another opportunity of victory, and, Christ being with us, another certainty of victory. Onward, then, ye Christian soldiers!

"Let your drooping hearts be glad;

March in heavenly armour clad."

Let not the brightness of your armour be stained by the rust of fear. You shall overcome as surely as your Lord has overcome. If you commit yourself to his keeping, and abide in him who is all-in-all to you, no defeat can possibly befall you.

I have this last word to add. There may be some here who will say, "Look, look; these Christian people have plenty of trouble." That is quite true; but they are not the only ones to be pitied: "Many sorrows shall be to the wicked." Those who are not in Christ Jesus shall also find tribulation in this world, for thorns and thistles spring up more numerously in the field of the sluggard than anywhere else. The wicked shall find that there are special sorrows for them—whips of scorpions for them, especially when they get farther on in life, and their youthful fires burn down to a black ash. Woe unto sinners when they have to reap the fruits of their evil deeds! O sirs, I would not have to go through life without a Saviour, as you do, no, not if I might be made an emperor. To have to fight this life-battle without Christ is sure defeat. What a discovery it will be when, having struggled through one life of sorrow, you shall find yourself beginning another life of greater sorrow, which will never come to an end!

It is an awful thing for a man to go from hell to hell; to make this world a hell, and then find another hell in the next world! But it were a blessed thing to go through fifty hells to heaven, if such a thing could be. It is glorious to struggle on through poverty, and sickness, and persecution, and to hear at last the word, "Well done!" That will be glorious! Who aspires to it? God help each one of us to labour after it, and give us strength to carry on the holy war, and fight it through even to the end!

But if you are wrapping yourselves up in these poor joys, these wretched rags of earth, and are living to make money, or to get drink, or to enjoy yourselves in the hurtful luxuries of lust, God have mercy upon you, and save you! Hear you the gospel, each one of you! "Believe on the Lord Jesus Christ, and thou shalt be saved." The Lord lead you to do so, for his name's sake! Amen.

# 6
# COMFORT FOR THE FEARFUL

*"He saith unto them, Why are ye fearful, O ye of little faith?"*
*—Matthew 8:26.*

*"Will He allow your present troubles to destroy you when so many others have not been able to hurt even a hair of your head? Trust in His love and dismiss your fears!"*

~

The winds were howling, the waters were roaring, and the disciples thought that the little ship must surely be engulfed in the raging sea, so they aroused their Master from his sorely-needed sleep, and cried to him, "Lord, save us: we perish." Note well the first words that he speaks to his frightened followers. Generally, when a man is in trouble, it is best first to help him out of it if we can, and then to give him any rebuke that he may deserve. Yet we may be quite sure that our Lord Jesus Christ followed the wisest order in every case. Being aroused because there was danger, he dealt first with the chief cause of danger; what was that? Not the winds or the waves, but the disciples' unbelief. There is always more peril, to a

Christian, in his own unbelief than in the most adverse circumstances by which he may be surrounded. Our Lord did not first rebuke the winds and waves, and then speak to the disciples; but he dealt with the chief peril first by rebuking their unbelief.

I think I may venture to say—though, to omnipotence, all things are possible,—that it was an easier task for Christ to calm the winds and the waves than to still the tumult raised by doubt in his disciples' minds; he could more swiftly cause a calm to fall upon the stormy surface of the Galilean lake than upon the perturbed spirits of his terrified apostles. The mental always excels the physical; the ruling of hearts is a greater thing than the governing of winds and waves. So, beloved, when we have to battle with trouble, let us always begin with ourselves,—our own fears, mistrusts, suspicions, selfishness, and self-will,—for the chief danger lies there. All the trouble in the world cannot harm you so much as half a grain of unbelief. Poverty cannot make you so poor as mistrust can; and sickness cannot make you so sick as unbelief can. The greatest evil to be dreaded is that of doubting your Lord. May God grant you grace to take this estimate of unbelief; and because Christ first rebuked that, and then the winds and the waves, so do you first seek to have yourself under proper control, so that, afterwards, you may be able to overcome your difficulties, whatever they may be. He who is, by the grace of God, enabled to master his own soul, need not doubt that he shall also be master of everything that opposes him.

I am going to try, as the Spirit of God shall help me, to minister consolation to any who are suffering through fear; and I shall speak, first, to *those who are Christ's disciples*, and who know that they are his; and then, secondly, I shall speak to *those who would not like to say that they are not his disciples, but who yet dare not say that they are*,—the many, who fain would be his, but who hardly dare to hope that he is willing to have them as his disciples. To them I shall say, as

Christ said to his apostles, "Why are ye fearful, O ye of little faith?"

**I. So, first, I shall apply the question in my text to those who really are the Lord's people,—those who are in the boat with Christ, his disciples, who follow him, and keep near to him: "Why are ye fearful, O ye of little faith?"**

First, *why is it that you doubt his love?* He brought you on to this stormy sea, he bade you take ship, and he knew all about this storm coming on. Do you think, because of your present experience, that he does not love you? You dare not utter such a calumny. Look back at your past life, and see how patiently he has borne with you. Your slowness in learning has not made your Divine Teacher angry, but he has still gone on teaching you. Do you remember when he first called you by his grace, and what you were when he called you? Do you recollect what you have been since he called you? Yet he has still continued to love you, and has not cast you away. Look back, I pray you, upon the many times in which he has appeared for you, bringing you through very severe trials, and sustaining you under very heavy burdens. After all this, do you mistrust him? Can you do so? Will you imitate the language of the unbelieving Israelites, and say, "Is it because there were no graves on shore that the Lord has brought us out upon this stormy sea?" Do you suspect that he has brought you thus far, encouraging you with many hopes, allaying your fears, and supplying your necessities, on purpose that he might overwhelm you with disappointment? Has he been trifling with you in all this,— exciting desires and expectations in you which, after all, are not to be fulfilled, but you are to be left to perish? Oh, no! each believer can confidently sing,—

"Can he have taught me to trust in his name,
And thus far have brought me to put me to shame?"

It is impossible that he can have done this; it is altogether unlike him, and inconsistent with all his past treatment of us, and with his well-known character. Come, child of God, you know that he loves you, after all. The proofs and pledges of that love rise up before your memory, so you cannot think that he will suffer you to be cast away. Will he allow your present troubles to destroy you, when so many others have not been able even to hurt a hair of your head? Trust in his love, and dismiss your fears.

Let me turn to another side of this truth. *Do you doubt your Lord's power?* These disciples ought not to have done so, for they had lately been eye-witnesses of many remarkable displays of his power. Had they not seen him cast out devils? Had they not been with him when a touch of his had healed the leper,—when, another time, the laying of his hand upon the fevered brow had raised the sick one from her bed? Had they not come fresh from a mass of miracles where, in the crowded street, he had dealt out healing to all manner of sufferers? How could they doubt his power when, before their own eyes, they had seen it so wonderfully displayed? Is he Master of devils, and not of winds? Can he cast out diseases, and not lull to sleep the roaring billows? It was both absurd and wicked for them to think of setting a limit to his unbounded power. And now, you dear child of God, after the experience you have had of his goodness, and after what you know the Lord did for you by his redeeming love in ages past,—dare you say that he has not power to deliver you now? Is anything too hard for the Lord? You say that you are poor; but can he not supply your need? Are not the cattle upon a thousand hills his own? Does he not claim the silver and gold as his treasure? He can feed the universe; he has done it these many centuries, and he is still doing it. The commissariat of the whole universe has depended upon his perpetual benevolence and care; and yet, from day to day, the hosts of birds, and beasts, and fishes, and insects, still are fed. And will not he, who supplies the wants of all living creatures by simply opening his hand, find food enough for his own child? Will you doubt his power? Is your case a very peculiar and difficult one? Do you draw a line, and say, "This God can do, but that he cannot do"? Is that right? Is it reasonable? Granted that he is omnipotent,—and he is omnipotent, whether you admit it or not,—and you have done away with difficulties. O thou with little faith in God's power, wherefore dost thou doubt? He can—he will—help thee, if thou wilt but trust him to do so.

Peradventure, however, your doubt may touch another point. *Have you any suspicion of God's wisdom?* Possibly, these disciples may have thought, "It was very unwise of our Master, just at eventide, to bid us cross this lake, which, lying low in a hollow surrounded by hills, is subject to very sudden and fierce gusts of wind, that catch a ship, and twist her round, so that no steersman can tell how to cope with the various currents and winds which are so extraordinary in their course. It was unwise of him to bring us here." Yet, if they did talk like that, they ought to have known better, for they had sat at his feet, and listened to the wondrous wisdom which poured from his lips. They knew that he was supremely wise; how, then, could they doubt? And dost thou, O child of God, think that the Lord is dealing unwisely with thee? Darest thou charge the all-wise Jehovah with folly? Whatever infinite wisdom does, must be right. Thou errest continually; what art thou but a mass of mistakes? What is thy life but a constant repetition of floundering and blundering? But he, who has shown his marvellous skill in creation, and his wondrous wisdom in redemption, and also in providence,—dost thou think that he miscalculates, or misses the mark he aims at, or that he can in any way err? Oh, cast away this dishonouring reflection upon the Lord, as thou hearest him say to thee, "Why art thou fearful, O thou of little faith?"

There are some other things which might very well have smitten the consciences of these fearful followers of Christ; and among them were these considerations which I suggest to you as worthy themes for your meditation. It is true that it was a terrible storm; but, then, *they were in the same boat with their Lord.* Whenever a foaming billow smote the ship, and agitated the breasts of the disciples, it moved their Master also. He had to bear all the tossing of the waves,—the wild leaping of the vessel from the billow's base to the billow's crown;—he must have felt it just as much as they did. If the little vessel went down with them, it must go down with him also, for they were in the same boat. How this thought ought to have lulled their fears to rest! And, beloved Christian, dost thou not know that he that believes in Jesus is sailing in the same ship with him? Remember how Paul writes, "For ye are dead, and your life is hid with Christ in God." "Because I live," said Jesus himself to his disciples, "ye shall live also." It was a bold saying of one that he had trusted Christ to save him, so he knew that he could not be lost. "But," asked someone, "suppose, after all, that you are lost?" "Well, then," he replied, "Christ would lose more than I should; for while I should lose my soul, he would lose his honour. If he did not save one who trusted him, he would lose his character as Saviour, he would lose the most precious jewel in his crown; and that can never be." No, he that believes in him shall never be ashamed nor confounded, world without end. He can never be either unable to save, or unfaithful to his promise to save all who trust him. Well does Dr. Watts write,—

"His honour is engaged to save
The meanest of his sheep;
All that his Heavenly Father gave
His hands securely keep."

Another reflection is that, although they were in a great storm, *the power that made the storm was the very power to which they had to trust.* There was not a single blast of the tempest but Jehovah's might had sent it, nor did a single wave leap up, in apparent wrath, but with God's permission, or at his command. It was his power, outside the vessel, that was putting them into peril, and they ought to have known that the same power would be exerted to deliver them. It is the same in your case; you are in great trouble, but does trouble spring out of the ground? Does it come by chance? Nay, God's hand is in it all. I know men talk of the laws of nature, but the laws of nature have no force in themselves; the whole force that carries out a law of nature is a divine force. So, your difficulties are of God's sending, trials of God's making, and they are all still in the hand of the all-powerful One to restrain, or mitigate, or increase, or direct according to his own will. You have often heard, I daresay, that pretty little story which I cannot help telling again, because it drops in so appropriately here, of the woman, on board ship, who was much disturbed in a storm, while her husband, the captain, was calm and restful. She asked him why he was so placid when she was so distressed. He did not answer in words, but he took down his sword, and held it to her breast. She smiled. He said, "Why are you not afraid? This is a sharp sword, with which I could slay you in a minute." "Ah!" she replied, "but I am not afraid of a sword when it is my husband who wields it." "So," said he, "neither am I afraid of a storm when it is my Father who sends it, and who manages it." Now, since all the trials and troubles of this mortal life are as much in the hand of the great God as that sword was in the hand of the good woman's husband, we need not be afraid of them, for they are all in his power. When he rides aloft in his chariot, and the skies tremble at the sound thereof, why should you tremble, even ye timid ones?

"The God that rules on high,
And thunders when he please,
That rides upon the stormy sky,
And manages the seas.
"This awful God is ours,

Our Father and our love."

It is only the flash of his spear when you see the vivid lightning, and only the roll of his majestic voice when you hear the thunders peal. Therefore, "why are ye fearful, O ye of little faith?"

There was another thing that ought to have kept those disciples from being afraid, and it was this. Suppose they had sunk,—still, having put to sea at his command, and with him on board,—*all would have been well with them*. I have heard of a sailor, who was very calm in a storm; and someone asked him, "Why are you not afraid? Can you swim?" "No," he said, "I cannot swim; but if I were to sink to the bottom of the sea, I should only sink into my Heavenly Father's hand, for he holds the waters in the hollow of his hand." That is a sweet thought; and if the worst comes to the worst with you, my brother,—if what we call "the worst" should come to you, my sister,—well, you would only die. You would go as low as the grave; but, blessed be God, you would never go any lower; and, in due time, even your body will come up again from that grave, and, re-united with your soul, be "for ever with the Lord," "wherefore, comfort one another with these words." But suppose you should die, your soul will then leap away from death into eternal life in a moment. Death would end all your troubles, rid you for ever of all your burdens, and you would be at home, to go no more out for ever, so you may well say, with good old John Ryland,—

"Come, welcome death,
I'll gladly go with thee."

There was one other reason why these disciples ought not to have been at all alarmed; and that was, *because their Master was asleep*. "Oh!" say you, "I do not see what comfort that was to them." Well, let me tell you what happened to me, one night, when I was on board ship. In my sleep, I started because I thought I heard something slip. Something had slipped; it was the anchor that had been cast overboard. I called out to one who slept near me, "What is the matter?" He said, "There is something the matter, I feel sure." "Why?" I asked, and he replied, "Because the captain is up." It was in the middle of the night, but the captain was up, so I was also up very soon, and saw that the captain was up, and that the sailors were quietly getting out a boat. If my friend had told me that the captain was asleep, I might have slept on, for I should have said, "It is all right if he is asleep. I need not trouble myself to know what is the matter;" but when I heard that he was up, I thought it was time for me to be up, too. If you were on board ship, and saw the captain busy heaving the lead, and doing it himself very deliberately and quietly, you would say to yourself, "I do not know what is wrong, but I feel sure that there is something the matter, the captain seems so anxious." But if, at any time, you were at sea, and you said to another passenger, "Where is the captain?" and the reply was, "Oh, he is in his berth, sound asleep!" you would say, "Oh then, it is all right! "Why did the Lord Jesus Christ go to sleep in a storm? Why, just because he knew that all was right; why should he not go to sleep? The great loving heart of Christ would not have rested if his children had been in any danger. It was because there was no danger, either to him or to them, that he went to sleep. Perhaps you are saying to yourself, "I have not had any wonderful deliverance from this trouble. I have had, in times gone by; but, now, the Lord does not seem to work any great marvel for me." No, because there is not any need for it. An old version of the eighteenth Psalm says,—

"On cherub and on cherubim
Full royally he rode,
And on the wings of mighty winds
Came flying all abroad.
"And so deliver'd he my soul:
Who is a rock but he?
He liveth,—blessed be my Rock!
My God exalted be!"
When the Lord thus descended from above, you may

depend that there was some great danger threatening one of his children; otherwise, he would not have come at such speed as that; and you may rest assured that, if he does not come thus to help you, it is because there really is not any urgent need for his interposition, as you are not in any great danger. Possibly, the Lord sees that it will be best for you to bear your troubles a little longer, for you are getting good out of them. He means to leave you in the furnace for a little while because he can see that your dross is being taken away; but if the good metal in you were being injured in the slightest degree, he would lift you out of the furnace directly. There is no serious harm happening to you, and, therefore, the Lord does not intervene. I hope that you can see now that the sleep of Jesus ought to have given rest to the minds of his disciples; but it did not, and he had to say to them, "Why are ye fearful, O ye of little faith?"

Thus I have spoken to the Lord's own people. May the Holy Spirit graciously bless the word to them!

**II. Now I want your attention, for a short time, while I speak to those who cannot say that they are Christ's disciples.**

There is a story told of Dr. John Owen, who was then Mr. John Owen, that he had been for two or three years in great distress of mind. He went to London, hoping to hear a very famous divine; but, on arriving at the meeting-house, he found that the doctor was not preaching. A man, whose name Mr. Owen never knew, preached from the text from which I am now preaching: "Why are ye fearful, O ye of little faith?" He was a man of no great ability; but it pleased God, that night, to break John Owen's fetters by means of the remarks that were made by the stranger-preacher, which were exactly suited to the condition of John Owen's mind at that time; and so, that mighty master of theology, perhaps the grandest of all English divines with whom God has ever favoured us, was brought into light and liberty through the instrumentality of that stranger-preacher. I wish that the few minutes, I can now spend in addressing you, could be as fruitful as his message was on that occasion. If only one of you is brought into the light, I will bless the name of the Lord; but I long for very many to be thus blessed.

You are seeking Christ, dear friend, and longing to be saved; but, for want of faith, yon are still in trouble of soul. What is your real condition? Perhaps you say, "*I labour under a deep sense of sin, I have been exceedingly guilty.*" Possibly, some one sin specially troubles you; or, more probably, a number; it may be that you know that you have sinned against light and knowledge, and you are aware of the peculiar provocation of having sinned, as you have done, after enjoying Christian teaching from your youth up. You feel that there is some special aggravation about your transgression, and you say to yourself, "I can scarcely believe that there is pardon for me." My dear friend, I put it to you, "Why art thou fearful, O thou of little faith?" Did not Jesus Christ come into the world to save sinners? Is there any sin which he is not able to forgive? It is true that there is a sin which is unto death; but you have not committed that sin, or else you would be in a state of death, and would have no desire to be saved; but if you have any spiritual life, so that you long to be saved, you have not committed that unpardonable sin, and all other sin and blasphemy can be forgiven unto men if they repent of it, and trust the Lord Jesus Christ. I am afraid that you do not think enough of the greatness of the Saviour,—that he is God as well as man. Consider the dignity of his person as God over all blessed for ever; yet, nevertheless, stooping to bear human sin! Think of your sin as much as you will, but do also think much more of the Sin-bearer, and his vicarious sufferings. Weep at the remembrance of your guilt; but weep on Calvary, weep with the wounds of Christ before you. But, oh! I pray you, do not do my Lord the great dishonour to say that he cannot forgive you. It is you who will not believe in him; it is, certainly, not with him that the difficulty lies. "He is able to save them to the uttermost that come unto God by him, seeing he ever liveth to make intercession for them. It is not possible that you are beyond his ability to save. There have been other persons saved, and many of them, who have sinned just as much as you have done; and even if there had not been any such, yet recollect that, if you are a sinner beyond all others, your case presents an opportunity for Christ to exceed everything that he has ever done; and he would delight in that. He delighteth in mercy; so, if you are really what you suppose yourself to be, namely, something altogether extraordinary in the way of guilt, then there remains room for Christ to show in you the extraordinary power of his grace. I pray you to believe that he can do this; trust him to do it, and you shall find that he both can and will.

Possibly, someone says, *"My difficulty is not so much concerning the power of God to pardon, as concerning the strong propensities to sin which I find dwelling in me.* How can they be conquered? I have resolved, a great many times, to overcome them; but I find my sin to be like Samson,—it is not to be bound with new cords and green withes, for it breaks loose from all its bonds. I cannot think that I can be saved with such an impetuous temper,—or such a proud spirit,"—or whatever form your sin happens to take. Now, beloved friend, it is well that you should see this difficulty; but is not he, who is mighty to save, quite able to grapple with it. Have you forgotten that text, "Behold, I make all things new"? Do you not know that the Spirit of God has been given that he may take away the heart of stone out of your flesh, and give you a heart of flesh? Have you never read the covenant of grace which says, "Then will I sprinkle clean water upon you, and ye shall be clean: from all your filthiness, and from all your idols, will I cleanse you. A new heart also will I give you, and a new spirit will I put within you." Is anything too hard for the Lord in this matter? I tell thee, if thou art near akin to a devil, he can make thee into something more than an angel; and if thy lusts and corruptions seem to have a strength that seems to thee to be well-nigh omnipotent, yet is the power of the Holy Spirit able to cast out all this evil, and to overcome the devil within thee. A strong man armed may keep the house; but when a stronger than he shall come, then shall he be driven forth, and be made to know who is his Master. Believe thou that Christ is stronger than thy sin, and come and trust thyself to him, O thou of little faith!

"*But*," says another, "*my trouble is, that I cannot find anything in me that Christ can work upon.* I perceive in my sister, who is saved, some traits of character that I think admirable; I perceive some redeeming feature in all converted people, but I do not perceive anything of the kind in myself. I seem to be weak where I ought to be strong, and strong where I ought to be weak. I am all that I ought not to be, and nothing that I should be." Ah, my friend! I want you to believe—to do my Lord Jesus the honour to believe—what he has a right to claim from you, namely, that he can deal readily enough with your case, for yours is just the typical case that he came to save. You remember God's ancient law concerning the leper who was to show himself to the priest. It was the priest's duty to examine him, from head to foot, with careful eye. While he was surveying him, he came upon a place, perhaps the size of the palm of his hand, where the flesh was perfectly healthy. There was no sign of leprosy in it whatever; and the priest said, "This is a fatal spot, you are unclean; you must be put away outside the camp." Then he examined another leper; and, looking him all over, though he seemed covered with scales of leprosy, yet the priest found that he had a little place, perhaps the size of the top of his finger, which was quite clear of the disease. The man said, "I have always thought there was hope for me, for you see that little spot, there is no leprosy there." But the priest sorrowfully shook his head, and said, "You are unclean; you must be put outside the camp." There came another leper, who said to the priest, "It is scarcely necessary for you to examine me; for, from the crown of my head to the sole of my foot, I am covered with this loathsome disease. There is not a speck or spot in me that has not the disease everywhere." So the priest looked, but he could not see one healthy place, and, therefore, he said, "You are clean; you may go wherever you like." I suppose it showed that the man's constitution had been strong enough to throw the disease out. I infer that was the *rationale* of it, physically; but, anyhow, according to the law of the leper, the man was clean; and, my friend, if, on looking yourself all over, you can perceive no good whatsoever, or anything like good, and if the great High Priest, even the Lord Jesus Christ, can see no good in you, he will pronounce you clean the moment you come unto him, and trust in him. This may seem strange to you, but it is the very essence of the gospel, even as Joseph Hart sings,—

" 'Tis perfect poverty alone
That sets the soul at large;
While we can call one mite our own,
We have no full discharge.
"But let our debts be what they may,
However great or small,
As soon as we have nought to pay,
Our Lord forgives us all."

Well, now, you who thus condemn yourself, should see that your very condemnation of yourself gives you hope of salvation. Why, the devil himself, I should think, would hardly dispute with some of you the fact that you are sinners. On the contrary, he has often been to you, and said, "See what a great sinner you are!" For once, he spoke the truth, though he did even that with an evil intention. If he says that to you, say to him, "Yes, Satan, you have proved that I am a sinner, but that is my hope of salvation, for 'it is a faithful saying, and worthy of all acceptation, that Christ Jesus came into the world to save sinners.' " He who condemns himself God absolves. He who is shut up in the prison of the law, so that he cannot escape; he who writes his own death-warrant, and signs it, and feels that he deserves to die,—he is the man for whom the Lord Jesus Christ sets open the door of mercy, and says, "Come unto me, for I have absolved thee. Thou art a free man. Be of good comfort. I died to redeem just such souls as thou art." So again I say, "O thou of little faith, wherefore dost thou doubt?"

Another case I would like to meet is that of one who says, "*Oh, but I have such a lack of sensibility!* I am afraid I do not feel humble enough. Some sinners weep, but I cannot. Some have upon them an awful horror of great darkness, but I have not; I wish I had." Dear friend, dost thou think that would help Christ to save thee? Oh, then, thou dost malign my Lord, who wants no help from thee! He can save thee, stony-hearted as thou art. If there be no sensibility, or anything else that is good about thee, he can give thee all this, or save thee just as thou art. Do not think that he needs thine assistance. What canst thou do, poor fool? I cannot help calling thee "fool" if thou dost think that thou canst do anything to help him to save thee. A righteousness like his,—wouldst thou patch thy rags upon it? Blood like his,—wouldst thou bring some bottles full of thy tears to add to the merit of his great sacrifice? I tell thee that the purest tear thou hast ever shed would stain his precious blood. Thou wilt need forgiveness for that tear if thou dreamest that there can be any merit in it to add to the merit of his blood.

"*Ah!*" says another, "*but I have to mourn my feebleness in prayer.* I know some, who have found Christ because they seemed to lay hold of him at the mercy-seat; but I cannot. I can hardly touch the hem of his garment." Well, then, do that; and if thou dost, thou shalt be healed. A little genuine faith ensures the death of all thy sin. Dost thou think that

Christ asks great things of thee? Listen, man. Though Christ bids thee look unto him, and live, it is he that first gives life to that eye of thine, or else it never could have looked unto him. There is nothing good in thee; it is all in Christ. From first to last, it is grace, *grace*, grace; and grace, you know, takes no payments, for it would mar its glory and its freeness if it took from thee anything from a thread to a shoelatchet. Be thou only emptiness, and Christ will be thy fulness.

"*But I do not feel,*" thou sayest. Well, then, be so empty that thou art even empty of feeling; thy feelings cannot save thee, but Christ will give thee all the feeling that thou needest. Come unto him just as thou art, and trust him for everything. You are like a child who has done something very wrong; and his father says, "My child, I will freely forgive you." The child says, "I cannot believe it; I have been so wicked; I want to do something." The father says, "My dear child, I love you so that I have freely forgiven you. I can forgive all, I can forget all, and I have done so." The child says, "But I know, if anyone had offended against me as I have done against you, I could not forgive and forget." "No," the father says, "but, my child, my ways are not thy ways, nor my thoughts thy thoughts." The child still cannot believe that his father loves him so as to be ready to forgive him; but if he would believe that, and just throw himself on his father's bosom with the cry, "Father, I have sinned," oh, what ease of mind he would at once feel! Out with thy confession! Let not sin be smouldering in thy bosom any longer. Tell the Lord how guilty thou art; tell him that thou deservest his utmost wrath; tell him that thou couldst not complain even if he should destroy thee, but tell him that thou dost cling to Christ, and to the promise of pardon made in his Word; say to him,—

"Thou hast promised to forgive
All who in thy Son believe;
Lord, I know thou canst not lie;

Give me Christ, or else I die."

That is the thing to do. God help you to do it! Believe over the head of your sins, believe over the head of your sensibility; and, I charge you, do not look at anything but Christ. When thou lookest on thy sins, instead of looking at Christ, thou makest an antichrist of thy sins; and when thou dost look on thy faith, and say, "I cannot think that my faith is enough,"—if thou lookest at thy faith instead of looking to Christ, I say, "Away with thy faith." Away with everything but what Christ has done, and what Christ is, and the boundless love of the great forgiving God, whose bowels yearn over thee, and who cries, "How shall I give thee up, Ephraim? how shall I deliver thee, Israel? how shall I make thee as Admah? how shall I set thee as Zeboim? Mine heart is turned within me, my repentings are kindled together, … for I am God, and not man." "O thou of little faith, why art thou so fearful?" Trust thy God, and live.

But, lastly, I hear someone else say, "*My trouble is concerning the difficulties of a Christian life.* How can I, if I begin to be a Christian, hold on to the end?" Dear friend, I will not deny that there are difficulties, and that they are very great,—much greater than you imagine; but your holding on is not the great matter; it is Christ who will hold you on. Your perseverance in grace is no more to be your own act, apart from Christ, than is your first hope in him. You are to look to Christ to be Omega as well to be Alpha,—to be the Z as well as to be the A of the Christian Alphabet; and if you come, and cast yourself upon him, it is not his custom to cast away any who come to him, neither at first nor yet afterwards. "Having loved his own which were in the world, he loved them unto the end." And he will do the same with you. He will subdue your corruptions, drive out your iniquities, and present you, at the last, "faultless" before his Father's throne. Oh, I can talk about this; but, after all, it is only the Lord and Giver of grace who can drive away your unbelief! May he do so now, and to his dear name shall be the praise for ever and ever! Amen.

# 7
# FAITH HAND IN HAND WITH FEAR

*"What time I am afraid, I will trust in thee."*
*—Psalm 56:3.*

*"May you, if you have fear, also have faith with your fear,*
*and then afterwards have your faith without any fear!*
*When faith gets strong enough, fears are expelled!"*

~

It must be a very difficult thing to be the first traveller through an unknown country, but it is a much more simple matter to travel where others have preceded us; however difficult may be the road, we discover our path by certain marks which they have left for us, and as we turn to the record of their journey, we say, "Yes, they said that here they came to a forest, and here is the forest; here they spoke of a broad river, and here they forded it; here is exactly the spot which is marked, we are in the right road, for we are following in the track of those who have gone before." Now God in his providence has placed us in "the ends of the world" as to time; a long caravan of pilgrims has preceded us, and they have left us marks on the way, and records of their journey.

A notable one among the pilgrims to the skies was David, for his pilgrimage was so singularly varied. Some travel to heaven amid sunshine almost all the way there; and some, on the other hand, seem to have storms from beginning to end. But David's case differed from these, for he had both the storms and the sunshine. No man had fairer weather than the King of Jerusalem, yet no man ever ploughed his way through soil that was more deep with mire, nor through an atmosphere more loaded with tempest than did this man of many tribulations. He has been a kind of pioneer for us. I remember seeing, some years ago, the French army going through Paris, and noticing some of the big, tall fellows, old men that had been in the wars of the first Napoleon. These went in front, and they seemed to be worth all the rest that were behind; they were the pioneers that cleared the way for the others. Now David, and such as he, of whom we read in the Scriptures, are the grand old soldiers that bear the standard and lead the way, and we are the raw recruits that follow on behind them. Let us be thankful that we have some veterans to lead the van.

Our text is rather an extraordinary one, yet it represents the experience of many of us, and we are comforted by the thought that our feelings and David's have very much agreed: "What time I am afraid, I will trust in thee."

You notice in the text, first, *a complex condition;* here is a man afraid, and yet he is trusting. Then we will look at *the natural side of this condition:* "I am afraid," and then we will look at *the gracious side:* "I will trust in thee."

## I. Notice, first, then, that here is David in a complex condition. He says, "I am afraid," yet with the same breath he says, "I will trust in thee."

Is not this a contradiction? It looks like a paradox. Paradox it may be, but contradiction it is not. What strange creatures we are! I suppose every man is a trinity, certainly every Christian man is,—spirit, soul, and body,—and we may be in three states at once, and we may not know which of the three is our real state. The whole three may be so mixed up that we become a puzzle to ourselves. Though certain mental philosophers would say that I egregiously err in asserting that such a thing can be, yet nevertheless I am quite certain that it is a very common experience of the child of God.

It is even quite possible for us to find two minds and two wills,—two sets of faculties within ourselves clashing and jarring and warring and contending with one another. In a record of some very notable experiences of doctors who attend upon the insane, there is a very singular case described of a man who was sane always regularly one day, as clear in the intellect and intelligent in judgment as any man; the next day he was always insane. On the day on which he was sane, he used to talk about how the doctor ought to treat him on the morrow, and to express his surprise that he entered into such a state, reasoning in the most practical manner. He seemed to be two men. There is a record of another case, even more remarkable, of a man who would act and speak and think as an intelligent full-grown person, but after sleeping two or three days he would wake up a child, to learn like a child, to talk like a child, to speak like a child, and to all intents and purposes to lead the life of a child. Then he would fall asleep again, and wake up as an adult person. To us it seems a most marvellous thing that this should happen; but perhaps it is even more marvellous to find ourselves perfectly sane, with no mental malady upon us, and yet at the same moment the subject of two opposite sets of feelings,— afraid, and yet trusting.

I am sure that every Christian here will follow me while, for a moment, I speak upon this singular duplex condition of *Christian experience.* You remember how the women returned from the sepulchre. They had seen a vision of angels, they had also seen the Lord, and it is said they departed quickly "with fear and great joy,"—very fearful, trembling at what they had seen, but very joyful,—never so fearful, and yet never so joyful before. And you remember that the disciples, when the Lord Jesus stood in their midst, "believed not for joy." Extraordinary thing! They did believe, or they could not have had the joy; and yet the joy seemed, when it grew out of the belief, to cut away its own roots, and "they believed not for joy,"—strange, marvellous state of mind, yet common to the Christian.

The same thing is true as to *our attitude to sin.* Have you not found yourself, beloved believer in Jesus Christ, drawn towards an evil thing for a moment, fascinated by it, finding a tendency in the carnal corruption of your nature to go after evil, and yet, at the very same time, you hated yourself that you should give way even for a moment to a thought so vile? You have felt the desire to go after sin, but yet another self, as it were, struggled with greater force not to go after it. One faculty seemed to say, "How sweet that sin would be," yet you have said, "It is gall and bitterness itself." The flesh has loved it, but the spirit has said, "I abominate it, I loathe it," and has cried out to God to prevent the possibility of our being allowed to indulge ourselves in it. Thus warring and contending with us, the prince of the power of the air, uniting with our own evil nature, has endeavoured to drag us down, while the Holy Ghost, co-working with the incorruptible seed which he has implanted in us, has sought to draw us upwards towards holiness, purity, and perfection. It is a wondrous warfare which only the elect of God can understand.

So, too, you have been the subject of another phase of this same phenomenon *in reference to faith.* You have seen a precious promise or a glorious doctrine, and you have believed it because you have found it in God's Word. You have believed it so as to grasp it, and feel it to be your own; yet, perhaps, almost at the same time certain rationalistic thoughts have come into your mind, and you have been vexed with doubts as to whether the promise is true. You remember, perhaps, the insinuations of others, or something rises up out of your own carnal reason that renders it difficult for you to believe, while at the same time you are believing. You battle with yourself; one self seems to say, "Is it so?" and yet your inner self seems to say, "I could die for it, I know it is so." You are tormented because you cannot answer certain arguments against it, but yet at the same time you feel that you have answered them, and that they are no arguments at all. Your heart repels all attacks upon the truth, and yet, somehow or other, for a while, you are staggered by the assault which Satan has made upon you.

I might go on to mention many other ways in which these two states of mind will come. I have found it frequently so *in prayer* when I have sought to draw near to God. An idle worldly spirit will bring ten thousand distracting thoughts to bear upon the soul, and the heart will seem to say, "I cannot pray just now, I have other things to do, I must think of them." What is worse, the mind will persist in thinking of these things, and they will come crowding in; some work that you have to do, perhaps some friend that you have to call upon, something you have forgotten,—these things will come pouring in upon you as if in your own heart you said, "I do not want to pray." Yet at that very same time you have felt a holy craving, an insatiable longing, to draw near to God in prayer, and you have said, "I must pray, I cannot live without it; I must now have a period of fellowship with God, cost me what it may." These two things will be there, the praying and the unpraying, the faithless and the believing struggling one with another, and your poor spirit will be like ground that is trampled upon by two armies that are fiercely contending as to which shall get the mastery. You see that in David's case, when in the text he says, "I am afraid," yet adds, "I will trust in thee."

## II. Now, secondly, let us look at the natural side of this condition.

David says, "I am afraid." Admire his honesty in making this confession. Some men would never have owned that they were afraid; they would have blustered, and said they cared for nothing; generally, there is no greater coward in this world than the man who never will own that he is afraid. But this hero of a thousand conflicts, this brave scion of the sons of men, honestly says, "I am afraid." Why was he afraid?

First, *because he was but a man*, and we men cannot rule the elements, we cannot overcome those who are mightier than ourselves. "They be many that fight against me, O thou Most High," he cries; and then he adds, "I am afraid." We cannot expect, therefore, that we should be free from fear when powers greater than our own are set in array against us. We are afraid because, at the very best, we are but weak and feeble men.

He was afraid, again, *because he was a sinful man*. It is this that makes cowards of us more than anything else. We know that we deserve the rod of our Father; and though, by faith, we feel assured that he will never use the sword of justice against us, yet we are often afraid that the correcting rod will be brought out, and that we shall be sorely chastened. Well, then, while we are men, and sinful men, it is no wonder that we should be afraid.

Besides, David was something more than that; he was afraid *because he was an intelligent man*. He knew his position, and could rightly estimate its risks. Now, with some persons, bravery arises from utter ignorance; they do not know the danger to which they are exposed, and therefore do not fear it. The unsaved sinner, if he did but know in what peril he is, would not be as quiet as he is. Unconverted men and women, if they did but know who and what and where they are, if they did but remember that "God is angry with the wicked every day," would be very ill at ease, they would be full of alarm and terror. But the Christian knows his position; he is not blind, his eyes have been opened, he has been brought to the light, he does not shut his eyes to the strength of his spiritual adversaries, nor to his own internal weakness, nor to the awful guilt of sin. He sees all these, and therefore it is not to be wondered at that, with so much of intelligence, as a Christian man he should have some misgivings. "I am afraid," saith he.

And then he is afraid, again, *because he is no stoic.* The heathen tried as far as they could to turn their flesh into iron, and harden their hearts into steel, but such is never the process through which the Christian passes. The Christian, when his sinews are most braced, and he is most heroic for his Master, is still as tender and as sensitive as a little child. The grace of God does not take away from us feminine tenderness, though it gives to us masculine courage; in fact, it blends the two in a perfect man, putting strength and sympathy together, and making us like to Christ who, with all the force of the majesty of holy determination and courage, had all the tenderness and gentleness that the fondest love could bring. Therefore we are afraid, because we do not boast of the insensibility of the Red Indian, but we still strive to be gentle and tender-hearted, the grace of God keeps us so.

But when is it that the saint should expect to be most afraid? Is it not when enemies around him are many? The psalmist, therefore, is afraid *because he is compassed by foes.* The Christian man does not like having enemies; if he could help it, he would not have a single one. He never willingly makes an enemy; and if he could destroy his enemies by turning them into friends, he would be delighted to achieve so great a victory. When, therefore, he sees that he has many enemies, and they are very cruel and very determined, then he is afraid.

We are afraid, sometimes, when we think of the old enemy, our spiritual enemy, for we know his cunning. He has been so long tempting the saints that he knows his business well. We know what poor, foolish birds we are when he is the fowler, how soon we are taken in his net; and, therefore, at the prospect of being tempted again by him, we bow our knee to our great Father, and we cry, "Lead us not into temptation, but deliver us from the evil one." We are afraid at the thought of having to fight Satan. Who that has read John Bunyan's description of Christian fighting Apollyon in the Valley of Humiliation but will feel afraid at the prospect of such a fight as that?

The man of God may be afraid, too, *because he sees want surrounding him*. The Christian must eat and drink, and though he is not to make this the great question of his life, yet he cannot look upon his little ones, and think that he will not have sufficient bread to fill their mouths, without being somewhat afraid. The natural side of the question must come up. He is not so hardened that he does not feel it; and when he sees want staring him in the face, for his own sake and for the sake of those about him, he is afraid.

If, in addition to all this, there comes upon him the remembrance of past sin, and with especial vividness some transgression into which he has lately fallen, he is afraid *because of the memory of the past*. Though he may look to Jesus, and he will do so, though he may see his sin laid on Christ, yet, even while he is looking, he will often be amazed with a sore amazement, and an agony of soul will come over him, not so much the fear of being finally cast away if indeed he be a child of God, but a fear lest, after all, he should turn out not to be what he hoped he was. If you never are afraid about the condition of your souls, I am afraid for you. If you never had a fear about your state, I think I may remind you of Cowper's lines,—

"He has no hope who never had a fear;

And he that never doubted of his state,

He may perhaps—perhaps he may—too late."

Under a sense of sin, it is but natural, nay, I will add, it is but right, that a trembling should come over the soul, and that we should fall down in the presence of God humbled before him.

The like is the case, too, with the man who is afraid *because of the thought of approaching death.* We have seen some, when they have come actually to die, rejoicing with joy unspeakable, and it has strengthened our faith when we have heard their bold declarations as they have felt the Master's presence in the final hour. But if, as a rule, you and I can think of death without any kind of fear, if no tremor ever crosses our minds, well, then, we must have marvellously strong faith, and I can only pray we may be retained in that strength of faith. For the most part, there is such a thing as terror in prospect of death; the fear is often greater in prospect than in reality; in fact, it is ever so in the case of the Christian. But yet, when we give ourselves up to fear for a time, we are grievously afraid.

This, then, is the natural side of the question. A man may be a true believer, he may be a very David, and yet be afraid.

### III. Now take the gracious side of it: "What time I am afraid, I will trust in thee."

"I will trust in thee." How glorious is this confession of faith! It is not the expression of nature, *it is a sign of grace.* No man trusteth in God unless there has first been a divine work upon his soul; at least, no man who is afraid can trust in God unless the Lord has taught his timorous spirit to fly like a dove to the sure dovecot cleft by divine grace in the Rock of ages. Happy soul that has been taught the sacred art and mystery of believing in Jesus! It is the highest and noblest of all the practical sciences; God grant us grace, what time we are afraid, to exercise ourselves in it!

It is a sure sign of grace when a man can trust in his God, for the natural man, when afraid, falls back on some human trust, or he thinks that he will be able to laugh at the occasion of fear. He gives himself up to jollity and forgetfulness, or perhaps he braces himself up with a natural resolution—

"To take arms against a sea of troubles,

And by opposing end them."

He goes anywhere but to his God. Only the gracious spirit, only the soul renewed by the Holy Ghost, will say, " 'What time I am afraid,' my one and only resort shall be this, 'I will trust in thee.' " The thoughtless, as I have said, try to laugh off their fears; the naturally thoughtful try to invent some scheme by which they may pass through the difficulty; but he who is truly believing leaves schemes and frivolities alike, and applies to his God with the burden of his care, and finds from him an instantaneous and effectual relief.

And, after all, *is it not the most reasonable thing in the world* that a soul that is afraid should trust in God? Where can there be a firmer ground of reliance than in him whose power never can be defeated, whose wisdom is never at a nonplus? If I have God's promise that he will help me, to whom or whither should I go but unto the God who has so promised? If, in addition, he has given me his oath, "that by two immutable things, in which it is impossible for God to lie," I might have strong consolation, where shall my timid spirit go but to the shadow of the wings of the God of the covenant who, by promise and by oath, has guaranteed my safety? What are my circumstances? Hath he not given me a promise suitable to them, a special promise for each special time? So I need never be afraid because of my circumstances. Has he not, indeed, given me one text which covers them all with its broad expanse? "We know that all things work together for good to them that love God, to them who are the called according to his purpose." With a God who is almighty and eternally faithful, with a God who promises, and seals the promise with his oath, that he will help me when I call upon him, what can be more reasonable than that, when I am afraid, I should come and put my trust in him?

Ah! my brethren, and as it is reasonable, *it certainly proves itself to be most effectual*, for he who trembles from head to foot does but begin to trust in God, and, behold, he grows calm at once. Have we not seen minds so distracted as to be almost bereft of reason grow quiet and peaceful when they have learnt to do the work they could do, and then left the rest to God? Oh! it is sweet waiting at the posts of Jehovah's door. It is well to tarry till his promise becomes ripe, and then in all its sweetness drops into our hands. "I will never leave thee, nor forsake thee," so hath he declared. My soul, lay hold upon that, and the next time thou art afraid, seek a safe shelter beneath that promise. "No good thing will he withhold from them that walk uprightly." When I am afraid lest I should be in want, I will come and get beneath that promise. If it be a good thing, God has bound himself by his Word to give it to me. "Fear thou not, for I am with thee; be not dismayed, for I am thy God; I will strengthen thee; yea, I will help thee; yea, I will uphold thee with the right hand of my righteousness." My God, when at another time I am full of alarm and dismay, I will come to thee, for thou art bound to strengthen and help and uphold thy servants who place their confidence in thee.

Dear brethren and sisters, let me exhort you—and may God's Holy Spirit back up the exhortation!—to the exercise of a holy trust in God, not only when you are happy, but when you are afraid. *Faith in God is a seasonable thing* as well as a reasonable thing. Fruit is always best in its season, and the time for faith is the time of trial. Faith is never so full-flavoured as when it is produced beneath cloudy skies. Other fruits need the sun to ripen them, but this is one of the precious fruits put forth by the moon. You shall, when your experience is most trying, honour God the most if you can then trust him. Surely, it needs little faith to believe in providence when the purse is full. What sort of faith is it that believes in the merits of the precious blood of Jesus when it feels its own sanctification to be complete, if such can ever be the case? What kind of faith is that which leans on the Beloved when it can stand alone? But that is true faith which, when it cannot stand by itself, which sees death written upon all its own power, which sees almost all its hopes withered and blasted with the East wind, yet cries, "My God, it is enough! My soul waiteth only upon thee. My expectation is from thee." This is the way to honour God indeed.

Observe the gradation there often is in Christian experience. You will sometimes find believers in so low a state that their heart is full of fear. By-and-by they are enabled to exercise the faith that God has given them, but it is mingled fear and trust. But they do not stop there, they get a little further, as David did in this Psalm, as you can see if you will read a verse or two further on; there it gets to be trust and no fear: "In God have I put my trust: I will not be afraid what man can do unto me." May you climb the steps of that gracious ladder! May you, if you have fear, also have faith with your fear, and then afterwards have your faith without any fear! When faith gets strong enough, fears are expelled.

Let me, however, return to my point that, when you are afraid, then is the time to trust the Lord. When you are very poor, then is the time to believe the doctrine of divine providence. When you feel the guilt of your sins, then is the time to lay hold on Jesus Christ, and to wash in the fountain filled with blood. Who cares to wash when he is clean? The time to wash is when the filth is felt; then fly to the all-cleansing blood. You say, "I feel so dead and cold, I have not the spiritual vivacity and warmth and life that I used to possess. I used to come up to the Tabernacle, and feel such joy and rejoicing in worshipping on God's holy day, but now I feel flat and dull." Oh! but do not be tempted to get away from Christ because of this. Who runs away from the fire because he is cold? Who, in summer, runs away from the cooling brook because he is hot? Should not my deadness be the reason why I should come to Jesus Christ? Now is the time for him to show his power. Now my Master, if indeed thou art a friend that sticketh closer than a brother, and, blessed be thy name, thou art such a friend, behold, here is one of thy friends; prove that thou canst forgive and still stick to him; cause him to trust in thee, and let him find thee better than all his fears.

I have done when I have made an application of my text to those of you who have not believed in Jesus, and yet desire to do so. I know your fears, your doubts, your tremblings. Let me whisper in your ear this word,—"Now that you are afraid, put your trust in Jesus. Christ came to save sinners such as you are with all your fear. Now, while your fears toss you to and fro, go to Jesus—

"While the raging billows roll,

While the tempest still is high."

Hang all your weight upon the Lover of souls now. Do not wait till you get rid of your fears, and then go to him; go now.

A lady was once walking in a field, and a bird flew right into her bosom. She wondered why the little lark came nestling there; but, looking up, she saw a hawk in the air; it had pursued the little bird, which, though it would have been quite afraid at any other time to find a shelter where it did find it, had by the greater fear of its enemy been driven out of the lesser fear. She to whom it fled for refuge cared for it, cherished it, and set it free. So be it with thee. Let thy great fears of hell overcome that fear that thou hast sometimes had, that perhaps Jesus may reject thee. Fly into his bosom. "Oh! but I fear that he will reject me." Well, then, I trust that your other fears will get so great as to overcome this fear. John Bunyan says that his fear of hell at last became so terrible that if Jesus Christ had stood with a naked sword in his hand, or if he had held a pike to him, he would have run on the point of the pike, and would always rather go to an angry Christ than be cast into hell. But, believe me, Christ is not angry. He holds no pike and no sword in his hand. This is his word of promise, "Him that cometh to me I will in no wise cast out." Aged sinner, you who have been a great transgressor, whoever you may be, if you come and simply cast yourself upon the blessed Saviour who on the cross offered up himself for human guilt, you shall be saved.

"What time I am afraid, I will trust in thee." I dare to say these ancient words to-night from the depths of my soul. I am afraid of my sins; I am afraid of my unworthiness; I never live a day but what I see reason to be afraid; if I had to stand all by myself, I should be afraid to stand before God. If I had never done anything in my life but preach this one sermon, there have been so many imperfections and faults in it that I am afraid to place any reliance upon it; but, my Lord Jesus, thou art my soul's only hope, I trust entirely in thee.

Beloved, have this same faith. May God work it in you, and then your fear shall only drive you closer to your Lord, and so the fear and the faith shall go on hand in hand together for a while, till at last perfect love shall come in, and take the place of fear, and then faith and love shall go hand in hand to heaven.

May the Lord bless every one of you, for Jesus' sake! Amen.

# 8
# REST, REST

*"Come unto me, all ye that labour and are heavy laden, and I will give you rest. Take my yoke upon you, and learn of me; for I am meek and lowly in heart: and ye shall find rest unto your souls. For my yoke is easy, and my burden is light."*
*—Matthew 11:28–30.*

*"Jesus Christ gives us in the gift of himself all the rest we can never enjoy, even heaven's rest lies in him; but after we have received him we have to learn his value, and find out by the teaching of his Spirit the fulness of the rest which he bestows."*

~

We have often repeated these memorable words, and they have brought us much comfort; but it is possible that we may never have looked deeply into them, so as to have seen the fulness of their meaning. The works of man will seldom bear close inspection. You shall take a needle which is highly polished, which appears to be without the slightest inequality upon its surface, and you shall put it under a microscope, and it will look like a rough bar of iron; but you shall select what you will from nature, the bark or the leaf of a tree, or the wing or the foot of an insect, and you shall discover no flaw, magnify it as much as you will, and gaze upon it as long as you please. So take the words of man. The first time you hear them they will strike you; you may hear them again and still admire their sentiment, but you shall soon weary of their repetition, and call them hackneyed and over-estimated. The words of Jesus are not so, they never lose their dew, they never become threadbare. You may ring the changes upon his words and never exhaust their music: you may consider them by day and by night, but familiarity shall not breed contempt. You shall beat them in the mortar of contemplation, with the pestle of criticism, and their perfume shall but become the more apparent. Dissect, investigate, and weigh the Master's teaching word by word, and each syllable will repay you. When loitering upon the Island of Liddo, off Venice, and listening to the sound of the city's bells, I thought the music charming as it floated across the lagune; but when I returned to the city, and sat down in the centre of the music, in the very midst of all the bells, the sweetness changed to a horrible clash, the charming sounds were transformed into a maddening din; not the slightest melody could I detect in any one bell, while harmony in the whole company of noisemakers was out of the question. Distance had lent enchantment to the sound. The words of poets and eloquent writers may, as a whole, and heard from afar, sound charmingly enough; but how few of them bear a near and minute investigation! Their belfry rings passably, but one would soon weary of each separate bell. It is never so with the divine words of Jesus. You hear them ringing from afar, and they are sweetness itself. When as a sinner, you roamed at midnight like a traveller lost on the wilds, how sweetly did they call you home! But now you have reached the house of mercy, you sit and listen to each distinct note of love's perfect peal, and wonderingly feel that even angelic harps cannot excel it.

We will, this morning, if we can, conduct you into the inner chambers of our text, place its words under the microscope, and peer into the recesses of each sentence. We only wish our microscope were of a greater magnifying power, and our ability to expound the text more complete; for there are mines of instruction here. Superficially read this royal promise has cheered and encouraged tens of thousands, but there is a wealth in it which the diligent digger and miner shall alone discover. Its shallows are cool and refreshing for the lambs, but in its depths are pearls, for which we hope to dive.

Our first head, this morning, is *rest*: "Come unto me, all ye that labour and are heavy laden, and I will give you rest." The second head is *rest*: "Take my yoke upon you, and learn of me; for I am meek and lowly in heart: and ye shall find rest unto your souls."

**I. Let us begin at the beginning with the first rest, and here we will make divisions only for the sake of bringing out the sense more clearly.**

1. Observe *the person invited* to receive this first rest: "Come unto me, all ye that labour and are heavy laden." The word *"all"* first demands attention: *"All* ye that labour." There was need for the insertion of that wide word. Had not the Saviour said a little before, "I thank thee, O Father, Lord of heaven and earth, because thou hast hid these things from the wise and prudent, and hast revealed them to babes"? Some who had been listening to the Saviour might have said, "The Father, then, has determined to whom he will reveal the Christ; there is a number chosen, according to the Father's good pleasure, to whom the gospel is revealed; while from another company it is hidden!" The too hasty inference, which it seems natural for man to draw from the doctrine is, "Then there is no invitation for me; there is no hope for me; I need not listen to the gospel's warnings and invitations." So the Saviour, as if to answer that discouraging notion, words his invitation thus, "Come unto me, *all* ye that

labour and are heavy laden." Let it not be supposed that election excludes any of you from the invitation of mercy; all of you who labour are bidden to come. Whatever the great doctrine of predestination may involve, rest assured that it by no means narrows or diminishes the extent of gospel invitations. The good news is to be preached to "every creature "under heaven, and in this particular passage it is addressed to *all* the labouring and heavy laden.

The description of the person invited is very full; it describes him both actively and passively. "*All ye that labour*"—there is the activity of men bearing the yoke, and ready to labour after salvation; "*heavy laden*"—there is the passive form of their religious condition, they sustain a burden, and are pressed down, and sorely wearied by the load they bear. There are to be found many who are actively engaged in seeking salvation; they believe that if they obey the precepts of the law they will be saved, and they are endeavouring to the utmost to do them; they have been told that the performance of certain rites and ceremonies will also save them, they are performing those with great care; the yoke is on their shoulders, and they are labouring diligently. Some are labouring in prayer, some are labouring in sacraments, others in self-denials and mortifications, but as a class they are awakened to feel the need of salvation, and they are intensely laborious to save themselves. It is to these the Saviour addresses his loving admonition: in effect he tells them, "This is not the way to rest, your self-imposed labours will end in disappointment; cease your wearisome exertions, and believe in me, for I will at once give you rest—the rest which my labours have earned for believers." Very speedily those who are active in self-righteously working for salvation fall into the passive state, and become burdened; their labour of itself becomes a burden to them. Besides the burden of their self-righteous labour, there comes upon them the awful, tremendous, crushing burden of past sin, and a sense of the wrath of God which is due to that sin. A soul which has to bear the load of its own sin, and the load of divine wrath, is indeed heavily laden. Atlas with the world upon his back had a light load compared with a sinner upon whom mountains of sin and wrath are piled. Such persons frequently are burdened, in addition, by fears and apprehensions; some of them correct, others of them baseless, but anyhow the burden daily grows. Their active labours do not diminish their passive sufferings. The acute anguish of their souls will often be increased in proportion as their endeavours are increased; and while they hope at first that if they labour industriously they will gradually diminish the mass of their sin, it happens that their labour adds to their weariness beneath its pressure; they feel a weight of disappointment, because their labour has not brought them rest; and a burden of despair, because they fear that deliverance will never come. Now these are the persons whom the Saviour calls to himself—those who are actively seeking salvation, those who are passively bearing the weight of sin and of divine wrath.

It is implied, too, that these are *undeserving* of rest, for it is said, "Come unto me, and I will *give* you rest." A gift is not of merit but of grace; wages and reward are for those who earn, but a gift is a matter of charity. O you who feel your unworthiness this morning, who have been seeking salvation earnestly, and suffering the weight of sin, Jesus will freely give to you what you cannot earn or purchase, he will give it as an act of his own free, rich, sovereign mercy; and he is prepared, if you come to him, to give it to you now, for so has he promised, "Come unto me, all ye that labour and are heavy laden, and I will give you rest."

2. Notice next, *the precept here laid down*: "Come." It is not "Learn," it is not "Take my yoke"—that is in the next verse, and is intended for the next stage of experience—but in the beginning the word of the Lord is, "Come unto me," "Come," "Come." A simple word, but very full of meaning. To come is to leave one thing and to advance to another. Come, then, ye labouring and heavy laden, leave

your legal labours, leave jour self-reliant efforts, leave your sins, leave your presumptions, leave all in which you hitherto have trusted, and come to Jesus, that is, think of, advance towards, rely upon the Saviour. Let your contemplations think of him who bore the load of human sin upon the cross of Calvary, where he was made sin for us. Let your minds consider him who from his cross hurled the enormous mass of his people's transgressions into a bottomless sepulchre, where it was buried for ever. Think of Jesus, the divinely-appointed substitute and sacrifice for guilty man. Then, seeing that he is God's own Son, let faith follow your contemplation; rely upon him, trust in him as having suffered in your stead, look to him for the payment of the debt which is due from you to the wrath of God. This is to come to Jesus. Repentance and faith make up this "Come—the repentance which leaves the place where you now stand, the faith which comes into reliance upon Jesus.

Observe, that the command to "Come" is put in the present tense, and in the Greek it is intensely present. It might be rendered something like this: "Hither to me all ye that labour and are heavy laden!" It is a "Come" which means not "Come to-morrow or next year," but "Now, at once." Advance, ye slaves, flee from your taskmaster now! Weary ones, recline on the promise now, and take your rest! Come now! By an act of instantaneous faith which will bring instantaneous peace, come and rely upon Jesus, and he will now give you rest. Rest shall at once follow the exercise of your faith. Perform that act of faith now. O may the eternal Spirit lead some labouring heavy laden soul to come to Jesus, and to come at this precise moment!

It is "Come unto *me*." Notice that. The Christ in his personality is to be trusted in. Not "Come to John, and hear him say, 'Repent, for the kingdom of heaven is at hand,'" for no rest is there. John commands a preparation for the rest, but he has no rest to give to the soul. Come not to the Pharisees, who will instruct you in tradition, and in the jots and tittles of the law; but go past these to Jesus, fine man, the God, the Mediator, the Redeemer, the propitiation for human guilt. If you want rest come to Christ in Gethsemane, to Christ on Calvary, to Christ risen, to Christ ascended. If you want rest, O weary souls, ye can find it nowhere until ye come and lay your burdens down at his dear pierced feet, and find life in looking alone to him. There is the precept then. Observe it is nothing but that one word, "Come." It is not "Do;" it is not even "Learn." It is not, "Take up my yoke," that will follow after, but must never be forced out of its proper place. To obtain the first rest, the rest which is a matter of gift—all that is asked of you is that you come to have it. Now, the least thing that charity itself can ask when it gives away its alms, is that men come for it. Come, ye needy, come and welcome; come and take the rest ye need. Jesus saith to you, "Come and take what I freely give." Without money come, without merit come, without preparation come. It is just, come, come now; come as you are, come with your burden, come with your yoke, though the yoke be the yoke of the devil, and the burden be the burden of sin, yet come as you are, and the promise shall be fulfilled to you, "I will give you rest."

3. Notice next *the promise spoken*, "I will give you rest." "I will *give*." It is a rest that is a gift; not a rest found in our experience by degrees, but given at once. As I shall have to show you, the next verse speaks of the rest that is found, wrought out, and discovered; but this is a rest given. We come to Jesus; we put out the empty hand of faith, and rest is given us at once most freely. We possess it at once, and it is ours for ever. It is a *present* rest, rest now; not rest after death; not rest after a time of probation and growth and advancement; but it is rest given when we come to Jesus, given there and then. And it is *perfect* rest too; for it is not said, nor is it implied, that the rest is incomplete. We do not read, "I will give you partial rest," but "rest," as much as if there were no other form of it. It is perfect and

complete in itself. In the blood and righteousness of Jesus our peace is perfect.

I shall not stay except to ask you now, brethren and sisters, whether you know the meaning of this given rest. Have you come to Jesus and has he given you perfect and present rest? If so, I know your eye will catch joyously those two little words, "*And I*," and I would' bid you lovingly remember *the promiser* who speaks. Jesus promises and Jesus performs. Did not all your rest, when first your sin was forgiven, come from him? The load was gone, but who took it? The yoke was removed, but who lifted it from off the shoulder? Do you not give to Jesus, this day, the glory of all your rest from the burden of guilt? Do you not praise his name with all your souls? Yes, I know you do. And you know how that rest came to you. It was by his substitution and your faith in that substitution. Your sin was not pardoned by a violation of divine justice; justice was satisfied in Jesus; he gave you rest. The fact that he has made full atonement is the rest of your spirit this morning. I know that deep down in your consciences, the calm which blesses you springs from a belief in your Lord's vicarious sacrifice. He bore the unrest that you might have the rest, and you receive rest this day as a free gift from him. You have done now with servile toils and hopeless burdens, you have entered into rest through believing; but all the rest and deliverance still comes to you as a gift from his dear hands, who purchased with a price this blessing for your souls. I earnestly wish that many who have never felt that rest, would come and have it; it is all they have to do to obtain it—to *come* for it; just where they now are, if God enables them to exercise a simple act of faith in Jesus, he will give them rest from all their past sin, from all their efforts to save themselves, a rest which shall be to his glory and to their joy.

**II. We must now advance to our second head— rest.**

It looks rather strange that after having received rest, the next verse should begin: "Take my *yoke* upon you." "Ah! I had been set free from labouring, am I to be a labourer again?" Yes, yes, take my yoke and begin. "And my *burden* is light." "Burden? why, I was heavy laden just now, am I to carry another burden?" Yes. A yoke—actively, and a burden—passively, I am to bear both of these. "But I found rest by getting rid of my yoke and my burden!" And you are to find a further rest by wearing a new yoke, and bearing a new burden. Your yoke galled, but Christ's yoke is easy; your burden was heavy, but Christ's burden is light. Before we enter into this matter more fully, let us illustrate it. How certain it is that a yoke is essential to produce rest, and without it rest is unknown! Spain found rest by getting rid of that wretched monarch Isabella; an iron yoke was her dominion upon the nation's neck, crushing every aspiration after progress by an intolerable tyranny. Up rose the nation, shook off its yoke, and threw aside its burden, and it had rest in a certain sense, rest *from* an evil. But Spain has not fully rested yet, and it seems that she will never find permanent rest till she has voluntarily taken up another yoke, and found for herself another burden. In a word, she must have a strong, settled, recognised government, and then only will her distractions cease. This is just a picture of the human soul. It is under the dominion of Satan, it wears his awful yoke, and works for him; it bears his accursed burden, and groans under it; Jesus sets it free—but has it, therefore, a perfect rest? Yes, a rest *from*, but not a rest *in*. What is wanted now is a new government; the soul must have a sovereign, a ruling principle, a master-motive; and when Jesus has taken that position, rest is come. This further rest is what is spoken of in the second verse. Let me give you another symbol. A little stream flowed through a manufacturing town; an unhappy little stream it was, for it was forced to turn huge wheels and heavy machinery, and it wound its miserable way through factories where it was dyed black and blue, until it became a foul and filthy ditch, and loathed itself. It felt the tyranny which polluted its very existence. Now, there came a deliverer who looked upon the streamlet and said, "I will set thee free and give thee rest." So he stopped up the water-course, and said, "Abide in thy place, thou shalt no more flow where thou art enslaved and defiled." In a very few days the brooklet found that it had but exchanged one evil for another. Its waters were stagnating, they were gathering into a great pool, and desiring to find a channel. It was in its very nature to flow on, and it foamed and swelled, and pressed against the dam which stayed it. Every hour it grow more inwardly restless, it threatened to break the barrier, and it made all who saw its angry looks tremble for the mischief it would do ere long. It never found rest until it was permitted to pursue an active course along a channel which had been prepared for it among the meadows and the corn fields. Then, when it watered the plains and made glad the villages, it was a happy streamlet, perfectly at rest. So our souls are made for activity, and when we are set free from the activities of our self-righteousness and the slavery of our sin, we must do something, and we shall never rest until we find that something to do. Hence in the text you will be pleased to see that there is something said about a yoke, which is the ensign of working, and something about a burden, which is the emblem of enduring. It is in man's mortal nature that he must do or endure, or else his spirit will stagnate and be far from rest.

1. We will consider this second rest, and notice that it is *rest after rest*. "I will give you rest" comes before "Ye shall find rest." It is the rest of a man who is already at rest, the repose of a man who has received a *given* rest, and now *discovers* the found rest. It is the rest of a learner—"Learn of me, and ye shall find rest." It is not so much the rest of one who was aforetime labouring and heavy laden, as of one who is to-day learning at the Saviour's feet. It is the

rest of a seeker evidently, for finding usually implies a search. Having been pardoned and saved, the saved man in the course of his experience discovers more and more reason for peace; he is learning, and seeking, and he finds. The rest is evidently lighted upon, however, as a thing unknown, which becomes the subject of discovery. The man had a rest *from* his burden; now he finds a rest *in* Christ, which exceeds what he asked or even thought.

I have looked at this rest after rest as being a treasure concealed in a precious box. The Lord Jesus gives to his people a priceless casket, called the gift of rest; it is set with brilliants and inlaid with gems, and the substance thereof is of wrought gold; whosoever possesses it feels and knows that his warfare is accomplished and his sin is pardoned. After awhile the happy owner begins to examine his treasure. It is all his own, but he has not yet seen it all, for one day he detects a secret drawer, he touches a hidden spring, and lo! before him lies a priceless Koh-i-noor surpassing all the rest. It had been given him it is certain, but he had not seen it at first, and therefore he *finds* it. Jesus Christ gives us in the gift of himself all the rest we can ever enjoy, even heaven's rest lies in him; but after we have received him we have to learn his value, and find out by the teaching of his Spirit the fulness of the rest which he bestows.

Now, I say to you who are saved, you who have looked to Jesus Christ, whether you looked this morning or twenty years ago, have you found out all that there is in the gift which Christ has given you? Have you found out the secret drawer yet? He has given you rest, but have you found the innermost rest which he works in your hearts? It is yours, for it is included in the one gift; but it is not yours enjoyed, understood, and triumphed in as yet unless you have found it, for the rest here meant is a rest after rest, a spiritual, experienced rest, which comes only to those who find it by experience.

2. Further observe that the rest in this second part of

our text is a *rest in service*. It is coupled with a yoke, for activity—"Take my yoke;" it is connected with a burden, for endurance—"My burden is light." He who is a Christian will not find rest in being idle. There is no unrest greater than that of the sluggard. If you would rest take Christ's yoke, be actively engaged in his service. As the bullock has the yoke put upon its neck and then begins to draw, so have the yoke of Christ put on your neck and commence to obey him. The rest of heaven is not the rest of sleep; they serve him day and night in his temple. They are always resting, and yet, in another sense, they rest not day nor night. Holy activity in heaven is perfect rest. True rest to the mind of the child of God is rest on the wing, rest in motion, rest in service, not rest with the yoke off, but, with the yoke on. We are to enter upon this service voluntarily; we are to *take his yoke* upon us voluntarily. You observe, it does not say, "Bear my yoke when it is laid upon you, but take it." Do not need to be told by the minister, "My dear brother, such-and-such a work you are bound to do," but take up the yoke of your own accord. Do not merely submit to be the Lord's servant, but seek his service. Ask, "What can I do?" Be desirous to do it; voluntarily, cheerfully, do all that lieth in you for the extension of his kingdom who has given you rest, and you shall find that the rest of your soul shall lie in your doing all you can for Jesus. Every active Christian will tell you he is never happier than when he has much to do; and, on the, whole, if he communes with Jesus, never more at rest than when he has least leisure. Look not for your rest in the mere enjoyments and excitements of religion, but find your rest in wearing a yoke which you love, and which, for that reason, is easy to your neck.

But, my dear brother, you must also be willing to bear Christ's burden. Now the burden of Christ is his cross, which every Christian must take up. Expect to be reproached, expect to meet with some degree of the-scandal of the cross, for the offence of it never ceases.

Persecution and reproach are a blessed burden; when your soul loves Jesus it is a light thing to suffer for him, and, therefore, never by any cowardly retirement or refusal to profess your faith, evade your share of this honourable load. Woe unto those who say, "I will never be a martyr." No rest is sweeter than the martyr's rest. Woe unto those who say, "We will go to heaven by night along a secret road, and so avoid the shame of the cross." The rest of the Christian is found not in cowardice but in courage; it lies not in providing for ease but in the brave endurance of suffering for the truth. The restful spirit counts the reproach of Christ to be greater riches than all the treasures of Egypt; he falls in love with the cross, and counts the burden light, and so finds rest in service, and rest in suffering. Note that well.

3. The rest before us is *rest through learning.* Does a friend say, "I do not see how I am ever to get rest in working, and rest in suffering"? My dear brother, you never will except you go to school, and you must go to school to Christ. "Learn of me," saith he, "for I am meek and lowly in heart." Now, in order to learn of Christ it is implied that we lay aside all prejudices of the past. These things much prevent our finding peace. Have you any preconceived notions of what religion should be? Have you fashioned on your own anvil ideas of what the doctrines of the gospel ought to be? Throw them all away; learn of Jesus, and unlearn your own thoughts.

Then, when you are willing to learn, please to note what is to be learned. In order to get perfect rest of mind you have to learn of Jesus not only the doctrines which he teaches, but a great deal more than that. To go to school to be orthodox is a good enough thing, but the orthodoxy which brings rest is an orthodoxy of the spirit. Observe the text, "Take my yoke upon you, and learn of me." What? For I am wise and learned, and can teach you? No; you are to learn from his example to be "meek and lowly in heart," and in learning that you will "find rest unto your souls." To catch the spirit of Jesus is the road to rest. To believe what he teaches me is something, to acknowledge him as my religious leader and as my Lord is much, but to strive to be conformed to his character, not merely in its external developments, but in its interior spirit, this is the grammar of rest. Learn to be like the meek and lowly-hearted One, and ye shall find rest.

He tells us the two points in which we are to learn of him. First, he is *meek*, then he says he is *lowly in heart*. Take the word "meek" first. I think that refers to the yoke-bearing, the active labour. If I actively labour for Christ I can only find rest in the labour by possessing the meek spirit of my Lord; for if I go forth to labour for Christ without a meek spirit, I shall very soon find that there is no rest in it, for the yoke will gall my shoulder. Somebody will begin objecting that I do not perform my work according to his liking. If I am not meek I shall find my proud spirit rising at once, and shall be for defending myself; I shall be irritated, or I shall be discouraged and inclined to do no more, because I am not appreciated as I should be. A meek spirit is not apt to be angry, and does not soon take offence, therefore if others find fault, the meek spirit goes working on, and is not offended; it will not hear the sharp word, nor reply to the severe criticism. If the meek spirit be grieved by some cutting censure and suffers for a moment, it is always ready to forgive and blot out the past, and go on again. The meek spirit in working only seeks to do good to others; it denies itself; it never expected to be well treated; it did not aim at being honoured; it never sought itself, but purposed only to do good to others. The meek spirit bowed its shoulder to the yoke, and expected to have to continue bowing in order to keep the yoke in the right place for labour. It did not look to be exalted by yoke-bearing; it is fully contented if it can exalt Christ and do good to his chosen ones. Remember how meek and lowly Jesus was in all his service, and how calmly, therefore, he bore with those who opposed him?

The Samaritans would not receive him, and therefore John, who felt the yoke a little galling to his unaccustomed shoulder, cried, "Master, call fire from heaven." Poor John! But Christ bore the yoke of service so well because of his meek spirit that he would do nothing of the kind. If one village would not receive him he passed on to another, and so laboured on. Your labour will become very easy if your spirits are very meek. It is the proud spirit that gets tired of doing good if it finds its labours not appreciated; but the brave, meek spirit, finds the yoke to be easy. "Consider him who endured such contradiction of sinners against himself, lest ye be weary and faint in your minds." If ye learn his meekness his yoke will be pleasant to your shoulder, and you will never wish to have it removed.

Then, as to the passive part of our rest-lesson, note the text, "I am *lowly in heart.*" We shall all have to bear something for the truth's sake so long as we are here. The reproach is a part of the gospel. The rod is a blessing of the covenant. The lowly heart finds the burden very light because it acquiesces in the divine will. The lowly heart says, "Not my will, but thine be done; let God be glorified in me, it shall be all I ask. Rich, poor, sick, or in health, it is all the same to me. If God the great One has the glory, what matters where such a little one as I am may be placed?" The lowly spirit does not seek after great things for itself, it learns in whatsoever state it is therewith to be content. If it be poor, "Never mind," says the lowly one, "I never aspired to be rich; among the great ones of this earth I never desired to shine." If it be denied honour, the humble spirit says, "I never asked for earthly glory, I seek not mine own honour but his that sent me. Why should I be honoured, a poor worm like me? If nobody speaks a good word of me, if I get Christ to say, "Well done, good and faithful servant," that is enough." And if the lowly-hearted have little worldly pleasure, he says, "This is not my place for pleasure, I deserve eternal pain, and if I do not have pleasures here I shall have them hereafter. I am well content to bide my time." Our blessed Lord was always of that lowly spirit. He did not strive, nor cry, nor cause his voice to be heard in the streets. The baubles of empire had no charm for him. Had fame offered to sound her trumpet for none but him he would have cared not one whit for the offer. The kingdoms of this world and the glory thereof were offered him, and he repelled the tempter. He was gentle, unobtrusive, self-denying; hence he treated his burden of poverty and shame as a light thing, "He endured the cross, despising the shame." If we once learn Christ's spirit we shall find rest unto our souls.

4. But we must pass on to notice, that it is very evident that the rest which we are to find is *a rest which grows entirely out of our spirits being conformed to the spirit of Christ.* "Learn of me, and ye shall find rest." It is then a spiritual rest, altogether independent of circumstances. It is a vain idea of ours, to suppose that if our circumstances were altered we should be more at rest. My brother, if you cannot rest in poverty, neither would you in riches; if you cannot rest in the midst of persecution, neither would you in the midst of honour. It is the spirit within that gives the rest, that rest has little to do with anything without. Men have sat on thrones and have found them uneasy places, while others on the rack have declared that they were at rest. The spirit is the spring of rest, as for the outward surroundings they are of small account. Let but your mind be like the mind of Christ, and you shall find rest unto your souls: a deep rest, a growing rest, a rest found out more and more, an abiding rest, not only which you have found, but which you shall go on to find. Justification gave you rest from the burden of sin, sanctification will give you rest from molesting cares; and in proportion as it becomes perfect, and you are like your Saviour, your rest shall become more like that of heaven.

I desire one other thing to be called to your mind before I turn to the practical use of the text, and that is, that here as in the former rest, we are led to adore and admire the blessed person of our Lord. Observe the words, *"For I."* Oh! it all comes from him still, the second rest as much as the first, the casket and the treasure in the secret drawer. It all hinges there, *"For I am."* In describing the second rest there is more said concerning him than in the first. In the first part of our text it only says, "I will give you rest;" but in the second part his character is more fully explained—"For I am meek and lowly in heart;" as if to show that as believers grow in grace, and enjoy more rest, they see more of Jesus and know more of him. All they know when sin is pardoned is that *he* gives it, perhaps they hardly know how; but afterwards when they come to rest in him in sweet fellowship, they know more of his personal attributes, and their rest for that very reason becomes more deep and perfect.

Come we now to the practical use of all this. Read the chapter before us and find the clue. First, my dear brethren, if you find rest to your souls you will not be moved by the judgment of men. The children in the market-place were the type of our Lord's generation, who railed both at John the Baptist and at our Lord. The generation which now is follows the same course, men are sure to cavil at our service. Never mind; take Christ's yoke on you, live to serve *him;* take Christ's burden, make it a point to bear all things for his sake, and you will not be affected either by praise or censure, for you will find rest to your souls in surrendering yourself to the Father's will. If you learn of Jesus you will have rest from the fear of men. I recollect, before I came to London, being at a prayer-meeting where a very quaint brother prayed for me that I might be delivered from the "bleating of the sheep." I understood it after awhile, he meant that I might live above the fear of man, that when such a person said "How much we have been edified to-day," I might not be puffed up; or if another said, "How dull the discourse was to-day," I might not be depressed. You will be delivered from "the bleating of the sheep" when you have the spirit of the

Good Shepherd.

Next you will be delivered from fretfulness at want of success. "Then began he to upbraid the cities wherein most of his mighty works were done, because they repented not." He had wrought his mighty works, and preached the gospel, and they did not repent. Was Jesus discouraged? Was he, as we sometimes are, ready to quit the work? No; his heart rested even then. If we come to Jesus, and take his yoke and burden, we too shall find rest, though Israel be not gathered.

Then, too, our Lord denounced judgments upon those who repented not. He told them that those who had heard the gospel and rejected it would find it more tolerable for Sodom and Gomorrah in the day of judgment than for them. There are some who quarrel with the judgments of God, and declare that they cannot bear to think of the condemnation of the impenitent. Is not this because they do not bear the burden of the Lord, but are self-willed? The saints are described in the book of Revelation as singing "Hallelujah" while the smoke of Babylon goeth up for ever and ever. We shall never receive with humble faith the judgment of God in its terror until we take Christ's yoke, and are lowly in heart. When we are like Jesus we shall not feel that the punishment is too much for the sin, but we shall sympathise with the justice of God, and say "Amen" to it. When the mind is lowly it never ventures to sit in judgment upon God, but rests in the conviction that the Judge of all must do right. It is not even anxious to make apologies and smoothe down the fact, for it feels, it is not mine to justify him, he can justify himself.'

So, again, with regard to the divine sovereignty. Notice the rest of the Saviour's mind upon that matter: "I thank thee, O Father, Lord of heaven and earth, that thou hast hid these things from the wise and prudent." Learning of Jesus, we too shall rest in reference to divine decrees; we shall rejoice in whatever the Lord determines; predestination will not cast a gloom over us, but we shall thank God for all he ordains.

What a blessed rest! As we open it up, does not its compass and depth surprise you? How sweet to lie passive in his hands, reconciled to every mystery, content with every dispensation, honoured by every service satisfied in God!

Now, I do not know whether I am right, but it struck me, when considering this text from various points, that probably our Saviour meant to convey an idea of deeper fellowship than we have yet considered. Did not he mean this—that he carried a yoke on his shoulder, which he calls "*my yoke*"? When bullocks are yoked, there are generally two. I have watched them in Northern Italy, and noticed that when two are yoked together, and they are perfectly agreed, the yoke is always easy to both of them. If one were determined to lie down and the other to stand up, the yoke would be very uncomfortable; but when they are both of one mind you will see them look at each other with those large, lustrous, brown eyes of theirs so lovingly, and with a look they read each other's minds, so that when one wants to lie down, down they go, or when one wishes to go forward, forward they both go, keeping step. In this way the yoke is easy. Now I think the Saviour says to us, "I am bearing one end of the yoke on my shoulder; come, my disciple, place your neck under the other side of it, and then learn of me. Keep step with me, be as I am, do as I do. I am meek and lowly in heart; your heart must be like mine, and then we will work together in blessed fellowship, and you will find that working with me is a happy thing; for my yoke is easy to me, and will be to you. Come then, true yoke-fellow, come and be yoked with me, take my yoke upon you, and learn of me." If that be the meaning of the text, and perhaps it is, it invites us to a fellowship most near and honourable. If it be not the meaning of the text, it is at any rate a position to be sought after, to be labourers together with Christ, bearing the same yoke. Such be our lot. Amen.

# 9
# RETURN UNTO THY REST

*"Return unto thy rest, O my soul;*
*for the Lord hath dealt bountifully with thee."*
*—Psalm 116:7.*

*"To miss even five minutes' communion with Christ,*
*is to lack an incalculable blessing."*

~

You, who have not believed in our Lord Jesus Christ, have no rest to which you can return, for you have never found any. May God grant to you the grace to come unto Christ, that you may find rest unto your souls! But we, who believe in him, do enter into rest. We are sometimes described as journeying through the wilderness towards Canaan, and the type is quite allowable; but, still, it must not be pressed too far; for, in another sense, we have already entered into our rest. We have entered the Canaan which our Joshua has given unto us; Moses, by the law, could not lead us into this promised land; but Jesus has brought us into it, and we now have our portion and our inheritance in the covenant blessings which God has provided for his people in Christ Jesus his Son. God's people, when they are as they ought to be, are in a state of rest even now. I do not mean that they will have rest so far as this world is concerned, for this earth is not our rest, it is polluted; but I do mean that, as the apostle Paul writes to the Romans, "There is therefore now no condemnation to them which are in Christ Jesus, who walk not after the flesh, but after the Spirit." I do mean that, as he also says, "Being justified by faith, we have peace with God through our Lord Jesus Christ;" and that peace includes "rest, sweet rest,"—especially that "peace of God, which passeth all understanding," which, the apostle declares, "shall keep your hearts and minds through Christ Jesus."

If I am, at this time, addressing any who have, for a while, lost the enjoyment of this blessed rest, my message to them is, "Return unto thy rest." I hope that they will be able to take the psalmist's words to themselves, and to say with him, "Return unto thy rest, O my soul; for the Lord hath dealt bountifully with thee."

**I. The first thing for us to remember is, that the believer has his rest. The psalmist says, "Return unto *thy* rest, O my soul."**

There is a position, or an experience, in which the believer's heart is perfectly at rest. While trying to think how I should describe it, nothing seemed to strike me as a more full and accurate description of the believer's rest than the apostolic benediction with which we are accustomed to dismiss our assemblies. He has true rest of heart who abides in the spirit of these words: "The grace of the Lord Jesus Christ, and the love of God, and the communion of the Holy Ghost, be with you all. Amen."

The first rest of the heart comes to us *through the grace of our Lord Jesus Christ.* We generally speak of him as the second Person of the blessed Trinity; but, in the benediction, he is put first, because, to our experience, he is first. No man comes unto God the Father except by God the Son; so, to us, Christ is first, because that is the way his grace works in us. And, beloved, when you know how to come to Christ for grace;—nay, when you have come to him, and have received from him the grace to cover all your sin;—the grace to justify you in the sight of God;—the grace of adoption, by which you become a son of God in him who is the Father's only-begotten and well-beloved Son;—when you have received the grace of union with Christ, so that you know yourselves to be members of his body, of his flesh, and of his bones;—when you know that all his grace is yours, and that he himself is yours, then it is that you get rest unto your souls. Sin cannot any longer disturb you, for it is drowned in the Red Sea of his atoning sacrifice. Your necessities cannot distress you, for they are all supplied by God "according to his riches in glory by Christ Jesus." Nothing need perplex, or afflict, or worry you any more. All the troubles of thought are ended as you believe what your Lord tells you. All the cravings of your heart are satisfied as you take him to be the Beloved of your soul. All the struggles of your conscience are ended as Christ brings to you peace and rest for ever concerning all your sin. In fact, as soon as you come to him, he gives you, through his abundant grace, rest about everything. This, then, is the first rest of the believer, which comes to him through the grace of our Lord and Saviour, Jesus Christ.

There is a further rest for us who believe, and a very sweet one; it is, *in the love of God*. It comes to us when we hear such a gentle whisper as this, "I have loved thee with an everlasting love: therefore with lovingkindness have I drawn thee;" or this, "Since thou wast precious in my sight, thou hast been honourable, and I have loved thee: therefore will I give men for thee, and people for thy life;" or this, "Fear not: for I have redeemed thee, I have called thee by thy name; thou art mine. When thou passest through the waters, I will be with thee; and through the rivers, they shall not overflow thee: when thou walkest through the fire, thou shalt not be burned; neither shall the flame kindle upon thee. For I am the Lord thy God, the Holy One of Israel, thy Saviour." Oh, what blessed rest springs out of electing love, and adopting love! What sweet rest we obtain from the assurance that God the Father and God the Son both love us, even as our Lord Jesus said to his disciples, "He that hath my commandments, and keepeth them, he it is that loveth me: and he that loveth me shall be loved of my Father, and I will love him, and will manifest myself to him." Thus is the love of God shed abroad in our hearts, by the Holy Ghost which is given unto us.

This glorious fact gives us rest with regard to our position here. We cannot be troubled by affliction, because it is sent to us in love. We cannot be worried about the future, for all its concerns are in the hands of the God of love. We no longer harbour doubt and mistrust, for we know that "God is love." O dear friends, when you once come really to know the love of God, it will give you wondrous rest! You will feel that he never smote a child of his except in love, that he never even frowned at one of his children except in love, and that he never was angry with one of his children except in love; and love, perhaps, never rises to a greater climax of affection than when it is forced to show its anger, and so uses the rod more to its own pain than to the suffering of those who feel it. Beloved, I trust that each one of you, who believes in Jesus, knows what that rest of heart is which enables you to say, "My God, my Father, thou canst do nought to me but what infinite love dictates, for I know that thou lovest me even as thou lovest thy firstborn and only-begotten Son."

The third rest of the believer is *in the communion of the Holy Ghost.* O beloved, this is the truest rest of the soul,—so far as your actual experience is concerned,—when the Holy Spirit comes, and takes complete possession of you, so that your will does not any longer struggle against the will of God, but sweetly yields to its control; your desires do not wander, but stay at home in full content; and you give yourself up entirely to the divine indwelling, so that Christ dwelleth in you, and you abide in him, by the power of his gracious Spirit. Then that same blessed Spirit brings to your mind the deep things of God, which are full of rich comfort for the soul, and the precious things of the everlasting hills of the covenant of grace, which abound in all the blessings that you can possibly want between here and heaven; for it is the Holy Spirit's special office to be the Comforter of Christ's people, and he makes the soul either to sit still at the feet of Jesus, to hearken to his gracious words, or else to run with cheerful yet restful alacrity on his errands, for there is such a thing as rest in running in his holy service.

Now, dear friend, if you have these three things,—the grace of our Lord Jesus Christ, the love of God, and the communion of the Holy Ghost,—I am sure I need not stay to prove to you that, in your experience, you have realized what it is to enjoy rest for your soul. Do you all know what it is thus to rest in the Lord? I thank God that I do; I feel, specially at certain times, that I could not ask the Lord for anything more than he has given me; I could not wish anything altered, I could not desire to be in any other state;—nay, I do not even wish to be in heaven at such times as those to which I am referring. When I sit down beneath his shadow with great delight, and his banner over me is love, and his fruit is sweet unto my taste, it is a little nether heaven,—the vestibule of the palace of the great King. Many of you must know what this rest is, I feel sure that you do.

**II. This fact makes it rather sad work to turn to the second division of my subject, which is that, sometimes, the believer leaves that rest. He should not do so; it is most grievous that he does; but, alas!**

**he does, as many of us are only too well aware by painful personal experience.**

Sometimes, he leaves it *through affliction*, and especially if that affliction comes from man. The psalmist tells us that, in his haste, he said, "All men are liars." Perhaps he said some other naughty things, for which he was sorry afterwards; it is not always easy to be calm and prudent when you are provoked, and to be quite restful when everybody speaks ill of you, or tries to lay traps to catch you. But the child of God should try so to master himself that all the dogs that bark can no more disturb him than the baying of a hound would turn the moon out of her nightly course. Happy and blessed is that man whose heart is fixed, so that he can sing and give praise even though his adversary is all the while speaking bitterly against him. Yet the flesh is very frail, and aches and pains of body, as well as cruel slanders against the character, will sometimes turn the Christian aside from his restful state. He is not quiet and calm; he is in a hurry, the leisure of his heart is broken, and he is in great confusion. God save us from getting into such a sorrowful condition as that! For, if we had more confidence in our God, we should have less confusion in our own experience. We should be much more restful if we did but do our God the justice of trusting him at all times, for he can never fail us.

I have known some Christians to be driven from their restful state *through a want of submission to the divine will*. O dear friends, when you have been in sharp trials, when things have gone awry with you, and, especially, if some beloved object of your heart's affection is taken from you, then you have had a quarrel with your God! It is a very sad thing that we should ever differ from infinite love, or think that we know better than eternal wisdom, or begin to suspect the grace of the Most High. It is sorrowful that this should ever be the case with any of us; and we cannot, without many tears, confess that we have sometimes had a dispute with God about what he has been doing with us. And then, of course, we could not rest; for, in addition to our other sorrows, our wise and loving Father chastised us for our naughtiness. He would not spare us for all our crying, but he went on with his own designs concerning us even while we were so wilful and rebellious. Perhaps he even chastened us the more because of that rebellion. We may be sure that we shall never truly rest in the Lord while we have a stubborn will; until every desire learns to lay its head in Christ's bosom, and is fully satisfied with him, we shall never be at perfect peace. There is, for each one of us, a modified agony and bloody sweat until, like our Lord, we can truthfully say to our Heavenly Father, "Not my will, but thine be done." That want of submission to God lies at the root of half our unrest. We must submit to him; it would be well for us if we did so at once.

Some Christians lose their rest *through want of contentment.* They are very happy in their present condition, for God has greatly blessed them; but their eye catches sight of a Christian who is better off than they are; and, straightway, they want to have as much as he has. They are not quite so well dressed as that brother is, and they wish that they were; their wife and family do not look, as the world says, quite so "respectable" as his; and, sometimes, in their folly, they will throw themselves out of a happy position in life, where they have the privileges of the means of grace, and go into a state of spiritual starvation just for the sake of being a little better off in temporal things, which is both foolish and wrong. Now, until we are perfectly content with what the Lord appoints for us, we shall not have rest unto our souls. Until we can honestly say,—

"To thy will I leave the rest,

Grant me but this one request,

Both in life and death to prove

Tokens of thy special love;"—

we shall never know what it is to enjoy full rest of heart.

I fear that there are many Christians who lose their rest in another way, namely, *through the world's joys*. Have you ever been, with a party of friends, where there has been a great deal of mirth and very little grace? If so, have you not felt, when you got home, that you could not pray as you were wont to do? Sometimes, you have been taking your recreation properly enough, but you have not carried Christ with you as you should have done; and you have found, after a while, that your rest has gone. Laughter and merriment may do you untold harm unless they are sanctified by the Word of God and prayer; if they are so sanctified, they may not cause us to leave our rest.

Frequently, too, Christian people lose their rest *through allowing some conscious sin*; for Christ and you will not long keep company with one another if you permit anything in your heart, or speech, or shop, or home, that is not according to his mind. His communion is with "the pure in heart: for they shall see God." But if sin be knowingly harboured, communion with Christ will not be enjoyed. The old Puritan was right when he said, "Sinning will make thee leave off communing, or else communing will make thee leave off sinning;" for the indulgence of any known sin is not compatible with a close walk with God. If, beloved, you and I get at a distance from God; if we follow Christ afar off, as Peter did; if we grow cold in heart, if we are neglectful of prayer, if the Word of God is not the subject of our constant study, if we get worldly and carnal, like so many of our fellow-Christians are, we shall soon find that the rest of our soul is gone.

It is a great mercy if you know when it is gone. It is a terrible thing to lose the joy of the Lord, and the rest of your spirit, and yet hardly to be aware that it is so with you. There is a very simple simile of this state of things, but it is a useful one You know that a hen, if she has some eggs under her, will keep on sitting. You may take half her eggs away, you may take three-fourths of them away; but she still keeps on sitting, for I suppose she cannot count. Now, there are some Christians who are very much like that hen; they lose the most of their grace, yet they are just as happy as they were before. But, beloved, your spiritual sense ought to be something much higher than the instinct of a poor silly bird; your care of the divine grace entrusted to your charge ought to be something far superior to the care of a sitting hen over her eggs. To lose a little grace, is to lose a great deal. To miss even five minutes' communion with Christ, is to lack an incalculable blessing. Therefore, brethren, if you have lost the blessed rest you once enjoyed, do not be satisfied to remain in that condition. Do not sing, with Cowper,—

"What peaceful hours I then enjoy'd,
How sweet their memory still!"—
unless you can also say, with him,—
"But now I find an aching void
The world can never fill."
Never be happy unless you are truly resting in Jesus.

### III. That brings us to our third point, which is, that the believer, when he has gone away from his rest, should return to it; and the sooner he does so, the better.

Return at once, dear friends, if you have gone away from your rest. As Noah's dove came back to him, so fly back to Christ, who is your Noah, your rest, for that is the meaning of the name.

And I would argue with you to come back, first, *because it is quite certain that you can never rest anywhere else.* A man, who knows not the Lord Jesus Christ, can find rest in many places,—such rest as it is. Give him a large estate, abundance of money, and plenty of worldly friends, and you will find him quite content with those things. Like the mole, which has its home in the earth, he will go and burrow, and make his home there. An eagle cannot do that; and you are one of God's eagles if you are a believer in Jesus Christ. Neither in wealth, nor in honour, nor in pleasure, nor in conjugal domestic comfort, can you ever find perfect rest. You have eaten the white bread of heaven, so your mouth is out of taste for the brown bread of earth. You might have been satisfied with the world if you had never known Christ, but you are spoilt for that now. A countryman, who has lived all his life in a lonely village, where he never heard any music, might be charmed when he first listened to one of our street organs; but let him hear some of the sweet strains of true music, then the noise of the street organ jars upon his ear, he cannot endure it. So, beloved, your ears have been attuned to something better than the world's merriment; that can never satisfy you. To you, there is only one rest; and you must come back to it. Some of you backsliders have come in here to-night; you have not been here lately, and you have been trying to be happy and comfortable apart from God; but, as surely as the Lord loves you, you will have to come back to him; and, the longer you stay away, the more bitter will be your weeping and lamentation when you do come back. Oh, that you would be wise, and return at once, and never wander away again! You know too much, and you have felt too much, ever to rest except in Christ, so do not attempt it.

Further, *this unrest puts you out of order for everything.* I should like to put the question to you, who love the Lord, but are not perfectly at rest in him,—Does not your present state very much spoil your devotions? You cannot pray as you used to do when you had such a sweet sense of the love of God; you know that you have not the power in prayer that you had, God does not hear you now as he once did. You used to run to him with your request, and come back with the favour you had asked of him; but, now, you ask many times, yet you receive no reply. The reason is, that you are walking contrary to him, and therefore he walks contrary to you.

Does not this want of restfulness also decrease your

power of working for Christ? You cannot plead with a sinner as you used to do, you cannot speak to the anxious as you once did; for, while your own soul is in the dark, although you may be wishful to give light to others, you feel that you cannot do it. If you wish really to serve the Lord effectively, you must have the joy of the Lord to be your strength.

Then, besides, do you not think that *your want of rest is putting you into a state in which you are very liable to be tempted, and to be overcome?* "The conies are but a feeble folk, yet make they their houses in the rocks;" and they are very sensible conies to do so, for there are many beasts of prey to seek their lives; but they run into the rock, and so they are safe. If you are out of your Rock, you are, like the coney, exposed to danger, so run back again as quickly as you can. You are never so safe as when you dwell in the wounded side of Jesus, peacefully resting in the grace of our Lord Jesus Christ, the love of God, and the communion of the Holy Ghost.

There is one thing more that I must say to those of you who are not thus resting; that is, *this unrest can do no possible good.* I say this to myself as well as to you, for I, too, have sometimes erred in that way. I am ashamed to confess that it is so, for it ought not to have been the case, and I feel that I am more guilty than some of you in having done so; but I never yet have found any good come of a state of unrest. When I have not rested in God about everything, I have never found things improve any the more for all my worrying. Suppose a farmer grumbles against God because the wheat is spoiling; does his grumbling save it? Suppose a tradesman begins quarrelling with God because business is dull; he will not bring one more customer to his shop by all his complaining. No; there is no good in grumbling, and no use in complaining; the very best thing that you can do for yourself is just to come back, and rest in God, and say, "It is the Lord; let him do what seemeth him good. I have done all I can that was right for me to do; but I know that it is vain for me to rise up early, and sit up late, and eat the bread of carefulness, unless he is pleased to send the increase. So I leave it all with him. I will not fret and worry any longer; I cannot improve matters if I do, so I will just leave everything in the Lord's hands." That is a right decision, my brother; for the end of your heart's controversy will be the beginning of your heart's rest. So, "rest in the Lord, and wait patiently for him." "Cast thy burden upon the Lord, and he shall sustain thee: he shall never suffer the righteous to be moved." "Delight thyself also in the Lord; and he shall give thee the desires of thine heart." But if thou wilt be unbelieving, if thou wilt rebel and revolt against thy God, thou shalt be smitten more and more, and no rest will come to thee at all. So, cry, with the psalmist, "Return unto thy rest, O my soul;" and not only say it, but do actually return at once unto thy rest.

**IV. The last thing about which I am going to speak to you is this. The believer has one excellent encouragement to return: "Return unto thy rest, O my soul; for the Lord hath dealt bountifully with thee."**

The psalmist tells us in detail what the Lord had done for him; or, rather, he tells the Lord: "For thou hast delivered my soul from death." In the fourth verse, he prayed, "O Lord, I beseech thee, deliver my soul." That was a single prayer, but he received a triple answer to it, for God is always "able to do exceeding abundantly above all that we ask or think." So the psalmist proved it, and he was able to say to the Lord, "Thou hast delivered my soul from death, mine eyes from tears, and my feet from falling." Now, believer, you ought to come back, and rest in God, because you have received from him these three marks of his divine favour.

First, *he has delivered your soul from death*. You will never die the second death. You are a saved man. As a believer in Christ, for you death has lost its sting. You may die, after a fashion; yet, living and believing in Jesus, you shall never see death in the full sense of that term. For you, there are no flaming fires of wrath, no pit that is bottomless, no curse of "Depart." Your soul has been delivered from death. Now, if that does not make you happy, what will? Why, my dear friends, the fact that God has saved our soul from death ought to fill our hearts with perpetual delight. Suppose I should be starved to death; still, it is a small matter now that my soul is delivered from going to hell for ever. Suppose I had to live in poverty and obscurity, and die like the martyrs at the stake; well, what of that? There is an everlasting crown that fadeth not away, that will abundantly recompense it all. "Strike, Lord," said Luther, "now that thou hast heard me. Do what thou wilt with me now that thou hast delivered my soul from death." I know how very poor you are, my dear friend, and what grievous burdens you have to carry; but, still, do not forget that the Lord has delivered your soul from death. You may be very poor, and very sick, and very sad, but you can never be lost. You may be laughed at by the ungodly, but you can never be cast into hell. Blessed be God for this! Surely, that is one thing to make you glad, and to encourage you to return unto your rest.

Next, the psalmist says, "*Thou hast delivered mine eyes from tears;*" and the Lord has done the same for many of us. We have no cause for grief now. "No cause for grief?" exclaims one. No; none whatever. "But I have lost my dear mother; shall I not weep?" Well, she loved the Lord; so she is gone to heaven; she is now before the throne of the Most High. So, if thou dost weep because thou hast lost her, then immediately begin to sing with joy because she is up among the angels. "But I have lost my little child who was so very dear to me." Oh, well! in that case, thou art mother to one who is praising God day and night; so wipe those tears away. I rather like the idea of a young person, at Brighton, who asked that she might have grey horses to draw her to her funeral. Why not? Why always have black ones? Why not have the white horses of delight? Let those who linger here sorrow that their loved ones have gone, but let them not be so ungenerous as not to sympathize in the eternal joy upon which righteous souls have entered. No; wipe your tears away, for "ye sorrow not, even as others which have no hope. For if we believe that Jesus died and rose again, even so them also which sleep in Jesus will God bring with him." "Oh, but!" cries another tried friend, "I have real cause for sorrow because I suffer so much, and I am so poor." Well, if it is so, it will all be over soon; and remember what the apostle says, "For our light affliction, which is but for a moment, worketh for us a far more exceeding and eternal weight of glory." "Yes," you say, "but, still, you do not know how much I suffer." No, I do not; and you do not know how much I suffer; but I know this,—if the two of us put all our sufferings together, they are not worthy to be compared with the eternal love of the blessed God who sent us all these aches and pains that we feel. They are all sent by him in love, so why should we cry over them? He has wiped our tears away, so let us not weep any more; or, if tears must come, let the salt that is in them tend to our sanctification; but do not let us shed one rebellious tear,—no, not even if all we have in the world were taken from us.

"Why should the soul a drop bemoan
Who has a fountain near;—
A fountain which will ever run
With waters sweet and clear?"

If I have all things, I have them in my God; and if all things are gone from me, I would find them all again in him.

Now, lastly, *God has also delivered our feet from falling*, as he did in the case of the psalmist. I know that one reason why many do not fully rest is because they are afraid that they shall fall from grace,—afraid that they shall dishonour their profession, and so on. Now, dear friends, I hope that you will never get rid of the godly fear of falling into sin, and never lose that holy insecurity with regard to yourself; but do not let that feeling extend to your God. You know that our Lord Jesus Christ said, "My sheep hear my voice, and I know them, and they follow me: and I give unto them eternal life; and they shall never perish, neither shall any man pluck them out of my hand. My Father, which gave them me, is greater than all; and no one is able to pluck them out of my Father's hand." He has delivered your feet from falling, so he will keep you. Therefore, begin to praise him and bless him this very moment. Cast away that fear of being cast away, and sing Jude's doxology, "Now unto him that is able to keep you from falling, and to present you faultless before the presence of his glory with exceeding joy, to the only wise God our Saviour, be glory and majesty, dominion and power, both now and ever. Amen."

No, you have nothing at all to fret about; your soul is delivered from death, your eyes from tears, your feet from falling; so rest, rest, rest, rest! You will glorify God by resting. One of the highest acts of devotion is to rest in the Lord. God grant it to you now, at his table especially, for his name's sake! Amen.

# 10
# LOVING ADVICE FOR
# ANXIOUS SEEKERS

*"If any of you lack wisdom, let him ask of God, that giveth to all men liberally, and upbraideth not;*
*and it shall be given him."*
*—James 1:5.*

*"To every honest Christian worker this text speaks with all the soft melody of an angel's whisper."*

~

If you are acquainted with the context, you will at once perceive that this verse has a special reference to persons in trouble. Much-tempted and severely-tried saints are frequently at their wits' end, and though they may be persuaded that in the end good will come out of all their afflictions, yet for the present they may be so distracted as not to know what to do. How fitly spoken and how seasonable is this word of the apostle, "If any of you lack wisdom, let him ask of God;" and such wisdom shall the Lord afford his afflicted sons, that the trying of their faith shall produce patience, and they themselves shall count it all joy that they have fallen in divers trials.

However, the promise is not to be limited to any one particular application, for the word, "If *any* of you," is so wide, so extensive, that whatever may be our necessity, whatever the dilemma which perplexes us, this text consoles us with the counsel, "If any man lack wisdom, let him ask of God."

This text might be peculiarly comforting to some of you who are working for God. You cannot work long for your heavenly Lord without perceiving that you need a greater wisdom than your own. Why, even in directing an enquirer to the cross of Christ, simple work as that may seem to be, we shall often discover our own inability and folly. In rebuking the backslider, in comforting the desponding, in restoring the fallen, in guiding the ignorant, we shall need to be taught of God, or else we shall meet with more failures than successes. To every honest Christian worker this text speaks with all the soft melody of an angel's whisper. "If any of you lack wisdom, let him ask of God." Thy lips shall overflow with knowledge, and thy tongue shall drop with words of wisdom, if thou wilt but wait on God and hear him before thou speakest to thy fellow men. Thou shalt be made wise to win souls if thou wilt learn to sit at the Master's feet, that he may teach thee the art which he followed when on earth, and follows still.

But the class of persons who just now win my heart's warmest sympathies are those who are seeking the Saviour; and, as the text says, "If *any* of you," I thought I should he quite right in giving seekers a share in it. They are seeking Christ, but they are in the dark: their soul desires Him, but it has little light, little guidance, and their cry is, "O that I knew where I might find him! that I might come even to his seat!" I thought that this text might be as the balm of Gilead to some of these unwise ones, who have found out all of a sudden their own sin and folly. I thought it would say to them, "If you, poor sinner, if you lack wisdom, seek of God who giveth to all men liberally, and upbraideth not." Let us put ourselves, then, at once in order for this work of comforting seekers, and may God, the Holy Ghost, make it effectual.

## I.  First, I shall call your attention to the great lack of many seekers, namely, wisdom.

This lack occurs from divers reasons. Sometimes it is *their pride* which makes them fools. Like Naaman, they would do some *great thing* if the prophet had bidden them, but they will not wash and be clean.

The natural heart rebels against the simplicity of the way of salvation. "What! am I to do nothing but simply accept the righteousness already finished? Am I to leave off doing, and merely to look unto Him who was nailed to the tree, and find all my salvation in Him? "Well, then," saith the proud heart, "I cannot understand it." It cannot understand it because it doth not love it. Now, soul, if this be thy difficulty, and I believe, in nine cases out of ten, a proud heart is at the root of all difficulty about the sinner's coming to Christ—if this it is which turns you aside and makes you foolish, then go to God about it, and seek wisdom from Him. He will show you the folly of this pride of yours, and teach you that simply to trust in Jesus is at once the safest and most suitable way of salvation. He will make you see that if the way of salvation had been by doing, the method would not have suited you, for what could you do? If it had been by feeling, it would not have suited you either, for what can your hard heart feel? How can you make yourself tender of heart? But, seeing that it is by faith, it is therefore by grace. O that you may be made wise enough to stoop and kiss the silver sceptre which is outstretched to you, to come and buy this wine and milk, without money and without price, and accept with your whole heart, with intense joy, this perfect righteousness, this finished salvation which Christ hath wrought out and brought in for every seeking soul.

Many persons also, are made foolish, so that they lack wisdom through *their despair*. Probably, nothing makes a man seem so much like a maniac as the loss of hope. When the mariner feels that the vessel is sinking, that the proud waves must soon overwhelm her, then he reels to and fro, and staggers like a drunken man, because he is at his wits' end. Ah! poor heart, when thou seest the blackness of sin, I do not wonder that thou art driven to despair; and when thy sins come howling behind thee, like so many ravenous wolves, all seeking to devour thee, I do not marvel if thou shouldst be ready even to lay violent hands upon thyself. It is no strange thing for men to be sorely tempted when they are under a sense of sin. And now thou knowest not what to do. If thou couldst be calm and quiet, we could tell you plainly the way of peace, and you might understand that there is no reason for despair, since Jesus died and rose again, and is "able to save to the uttermost them that come unto God by him;" but you cannot give us a calm hearing, for you are distracted, and you think that this comfort applies to everybody but you. You lack wisdom because you are in such a worry and turmoil. As John Bunyan used to say, you are much troubled up and down in your thoughts. I pray you, then, ask wisdom of God, and even out of the depths if you cry unto him, he will be pleased to instruct you and bring you out into a safe way.

No doubt many other persons lack wisdom because they are *not instructed in gospel doctrine*. It is wonderful how Satan will plague many timid hearts with the doctrine of election. That doctrine, rightly understood, is full of comfort; but, distorted and misrepresented, it often appears to be a bolt to shut sinners out from mercy—the fact being that it shuts none out, but shuts tens of thousands in. Why, the very doctrine of the atonement is not understood by many, while they are under a sense of sin. If they could see that Christ took their sins and carried their sorrows; if they could perceive the meaning of that word, "substitution," light might break in. The window of the understanding is blocked up with ignorance, if we could but clean away the cobwebs and filth, then might the light of the knowledge of Christ come streaming in, and they might rejoice in his salvation. Well, dear friends, if you are be-mired and be-puzzled with difficult doctrine, the text comes to you and says, "If any man lack wisdom, let him ask of God."

*Ignorance also of Christian experience* is another cause for the lack of wisdom. I have seen many enquirers who have told me what they have felt, and to them it was so amazing, that they half expected to see every individual hair of my head stand upright while they told me their feelings; and when I said, "Oh! yes, yes, I have felt just that; that is the common way of most souls that come to Christ;" they have looked surprised beyond measure. The very road which is most safe, you think to be most dangerous; and that which leads to Christ, you fancy leads to hell. Little do ye know the value of that stripping work which you so much dread. "Surely," say you, "I am being stripped that I may be cast away;" whereas the Lord only strips those whom he intends afterwards to clothe with the robe of his salvation. Those cuttings of the lancet are sharp, and you think the surgeon means to kill, but he intends to cure. When God is making you feel the burden of your guilt, you suppose that now he has forgotten to be gracious, whereas it is now that he is gracious to you in very deed, and is using the best means of making you understand and value his grace. The way of life is a new road to you, poor seeking soul, and therefore you lack wisdom in it and make many mistakes about it. The text lovingly advises, "Ask of God;" "Ask of God."

Very likely, in addition to all this, which may well enough make you lack wisdom, there are *certain singularities in the action of providence towards you*, which fill you with dismay. Ever since you have begun to think about the Lord Jesus, things have gone cross with you in the outward world. You have not only trouble within, but, strange as you think it is, you have now trouble without: it partly arises from friends who say you are mad—would God they were bitten with the same madness!—partly from circumstances over which you can have no control. It is not at all unusual for God to make a complete shipwreck of that vessel in which his people sail, although he fulfils his promise, that not a hair of their heads shall perish. I should not wonder if he would cause two seas to meet around your barque, so that there should not be more than a few boards and broken pieces of the ship left to you, but oh! if you have faith in Christ, he will certainly bring you safe to shore. It is not at all an uncommon thing for the Lord to add to the inward scourgings of conscience the outward lashings of affliction. These double scourgings are meant for proud, stubborn hearts, that they may be humbly brought to Jesus' feet, for of us it may be said, in truth, as Solomon saith of the child, "Foolishness is bound in his heart; but the rod of correction shall drive it far from him." God is thus, dear hearer, bringing folly out of you by the smarts of his rod. It is written, "The blueness of a wound cleanseth away evil," and therefore the Lord is making your wounds to be black and blue, and I should not wonder if he will even let them putrefy, till you have to say with Isaiah, "From the sole of the foot even unto the head there is no soundness in it; but wounds, and bruises, and putrifying sores." Then it is that eternal mercy will take advantage of your dire extremity, and your deep distress shall bring you to Christ who never would have been brought by any other means.

To close this somewhat painful picture. Many lack wisdom because in addition to all their fears and their ignorance, they are fiercely attacked by *Satan*. John Bunyan tells us of Apollyon, that he said, "No king will willingly lose his subjects." Of course, he will not; and Apollyon, as he sees his subjects one after another desert him to enlist under the banner of King Jesus, howls at his losses, and he leaves no stone unturned to keep souls back from mercy. Just at that critical moment when the soul is beginning to turn to God, he says to himself, "It is now or never. If I do not nip these buds, they will become flowers and fruits; but if I can bring in a withering frost, I shall kill the young plant." The great enemy makes a dead set at anxious souls. He it is who digs that Slough of Despond right in front of the wicket gate, and keeps the big dog to howl before the door, so that poor trembling Mercy may go into a fainting fit, and find herself too weak to knock at the door. "Now," saith he to all his servants, "shoot your arrows at that awakened soul; it is about to escape from me: empty your quivers, ye soldiers of the pit; launch your hot temptations, ye fiends of hell! Sting that soul with infidel insinuations and hideous blasphemies, for if I once lose it I have lost it for ever; therefore, hold it, ye princes of the pit, hold it fast, if ye can." Now, in such a plight as that, with your foolish heart, and the wicked world, and the evil one, and your sins in dreadful alliance to destroy you, what could such a poor timid one as you do, if it were not for this precious word, "If any of *you*"—that must mean you—"If any of you lack wisdom, let him ask of God, that giveth to all men liberally, and upbraideth not"?

## II. We shall now mention the second point in the text. The proper place of a seeker's resort—"*Let him ask of God.*"

My dear friends, bear me witness that it is my constant effort to teach you the spirituality of true religion, and the necessity of our own hearts having personal dealings with the living God. Now, though this you have heard thousands of times, I was about to say from me, yet, once again, I must remind you of it: the text says, "Let him ask *of God.*" Now, you perceive, that the man is directed at once to God, without any intermediate object, or ceremony, or person. You are not told here to seek direction from good books; they may become very useful as auxiliary helps, but the best of human books, if followed slavishly, will mislead. For instance, I am sure that hundreds of persons have been kept in unnecessary bondage through that wonderful and admirable book, "Doddridge's Rise and Progress of Religion in the Soul." It has been the means of the conversion of hundreds; it has been profitable to thousands more; but there is a point in which it fails, so that, if you slavishly follow it, you may read the book through, and I undertake to say, you will not find comfort by following its exhortations. It fails, as all human guides must, if we trust in them and forget the Great Shepherd of Israel. When a man is really under concern of soul, he is in a condition of considerable danger. Then it is that an artful false teacher may get hold of him, and cozen him into heresy and unscriptural doctrine. Hence the text does not say, "If any man lack wisdom, let him ask his priest;" that is about the worst thing he can do; for he who sets himself up for a priest, is either a deceiver or deceived. "Let him ask of God," that is the advice of the Scripture. We are all so ready to go to books, to go to men, to go to ceremonies, to anything except to God. Man will worship God with his eyes, and his arms, and his knees, and his mouth—with anything but his heart—and we are all of us anxious, more or less, until we are renewed by grace, to get off the heart-worship of God. Juan de Valdey says, that, "Just as an ignorant man takes a crucifix and says, 'This crucifix will help me to think of Christ,' so he bows before it and never does think of Christ at all, but stops short at the crucifix; so," says he, "the learned man takes his book and says, 'This book will teach me the mysteries of the kingdom,' but instead of giving his thoughts to the mysteries of godliness, he reads his book mechanically and stops at the book, instead of meditating and diving into the truth." It is the action of the mind that God accepts, not the motion of the body; it is the thought communing with him; it is the soul coming into contact with the soul of God; it is spirit-worship which the Lord accepts. Consequently, the text does not say, "Let him ask books," nor "ask priests," but, "let him ask of God."

Above all, do not let the seeker ask of himself and follow his own imaginings and feelings. All human guides are bad, but you yourself will be your own worst guide. "Let him ask *of God.*" When a man can fairly and honestly say, "I have bowed the knee unto the Lord God of Israel, and asked him, for Jesus' sake, to guide me and to direct me by his Spirit, and then I turned to the Book of God, asking God to be my guide into the book," I cannot believe but what such a man will soon obtain saving wisdom.

I beg to caution all of you against stopping short of really asking *of God.* I conjure you by the living God, do not be satisfied with asking of me. I am no priest, except as all believers are priests, thank God. I wear no title of ecclesiastical dominion. Be not content with asking my brethren, the deacons and elders: God has made many of them wise in helping souls out of difficulties; do not be satisfied with the advice of any man, however godly and holy, but go direct to the Lord God of heaven and earth, and say unto him, "Lord, teach thou me! Show me thy way, O God! Teach me in thy truth!" You are not bidden to go to any second-hand source of wisdom, but to God the only wise, who alone can direct you. "Let him ask of God."

Such advice as this must be good. You cannot suspect us of any interested motive in exhorting you to this. It is your good which we seek, and not our own glory. It must be best to go to head-quarters: you will surely be led aright if so you seek direction. Some say, Lo, here! others say, Lo, there! but if you go to God, and then with his guidance study his word, you shall not fail of wisdom. How can you?

Moreover, remember that there is one blessed person

of the divine Unity who makes it his especial office to teach us! Hence, if you go to God for wisdom, you only go for that which it is his nature and his office to give. The Holy Ghost is given to this end: "He shall teach you all things, and bring all things to your remembrance, whatsoever I have said unto you." When you go to God, you may say to him these words, "O Father, thou hast been pleased to reveal to us the Holy Spirit, who is to lighten our darkness, and to remove our ignorance. Oh, let that Spirit of thine dwell in me; I am willing to be taught by thy Spirit, through thy word, or through thy ministers, but I come first to thee because I know that thy word and thy ministers, apart from thyself, cannot teach me anything. O Lord, teach thou me." I do not mean by any word of mine to make you think little of Scripture—God forbid!—nor little of those who may speak to you with the Holy Ghost sent down from heaven, but I did mean to make you look even at that Book, and at God's ministers, as being subservient to the Holy Ghost himself. Go to him; ask him: for there in the Book is the letter which killeth; he, he alone can make you to know the living essence and the quickening power of that word. Without the Holy Ghost, my dear hearer, you must still be as blind with the light as you would have been without it. You will be as foolish after having been taught the gospel in the theory of it, as you were before you knew it. Let the Holy Spirit, however, teach you, and you shall know all things that are necessary for this life and godliness.

Thus, then, we have brought two points before you: the great lack of the seeker is "wisdom;" and the right place to get that lack removed.

### III. Thirdly, the right mode in which to go to God. "*Let him ask.*"

Oh! that simple word, "Let him *ask*"—"let him *ask!*" No form of asking is prescribed, no words laid down, no method dictated, no hour set apart, no rubric printed; but there it stands in gracious simplicity, "let him *ask*."

He who will not have mercy when it is to be had for the asking for, deserves to die without it. While I am thinking of this word, before I plunge into its fullest meaning, I may well say, if God will give wisdom to the seeker only because he asks for it, what shall I say of the folly which will not even ask to be *made* wise? May God forgive you such folly for the past, and deliver you from it for the future.

The text says, "Let him ask," which is a method implying that *ignorance is confessed*. No man will ask wisdom till he knows that he is ignorant. Come, dear hearer, confess your ignorance into the ear of God, who is as present here as you are; say unto him, "Lord, I have discovered now that I am not so wise as I thought I was; I am foolish and vain. Lord, teach thou me." Make a full confession, and this shall be a good beginning for prayer.

Asking has also in it the fact that *God is believed in*. We *cannot* ask of a person of whose existence we have any doubt, and we *will not* ask of a person of whose hearing us we have serious suspicions. Who would stand in the desert of Sahara and cry aloud, where there is no living ear to hear? Now, my dear hearer, thou believest that there is a God. Ask, then! Dost thou not believe that he is here, that he will hear thy cry, that he will be pleased in answer to thy cry to give thee what thou askest for? Now, if thou canst believe that there is a God, that he is here and that he will hear thee, then confess thy ignorance, and ask him now to give thee the promised wisdom for Jesus' sake.

There is in this method of approaching God by asking, also, *a clear sight that salvation is by grace*. It does not say, "Let him buy of God, let him demand of God, let him earn from God." Oh! no—"let him ask of God." It is the beggar's word. The beggar asks an alms. You are to ask as the beggar asks of you in the street, and God will give to you far more liberally than you give to the poor. You must confess that you have no merit of your own. If you will not acknowledge that, neither will God hear your prayers; but come now with the acknowledgment of ignorance, with the confession of sin, and believing that God is the rewarder of them that diligently seek him, and he will even now give you the wisdom which saves the soul.

Observe here, what *an acknowledgement of dependence* there is. The man sees that he cannot find wisdom anywhere else, but that it must come from God. He turns his eye to the only fountain, and leaves the broken cisterns. Do this, dear hearer. I feel as if the text did not want any explanation from me, but only wanted carrying out by you. Let him ask of God. I think I can hear fifty-thousand objections from different parts of the building. One is saying, "But I don't understand, ask of God." Another is saying, "I cannot comprehend, ask of God." If thou hast made some difficulties for thyself, if thou art such a fool as to be tying knots and wanting to get them untied before thou wilt believe in Jesus, then I have nothing to say to thee, except it were, beware lest thou dost tie a knot that shall destroy thy soul; but if thou be troubled with an honest objection, I say to thee *now*, in God's name, "*Ask of God.*" You need not wait till you get home, you need not stay till you have left that seat, but now, silently, in your soul, as Hannah did when she went up to the tabernacle, breathe the prayer, "O God, teach thou me: lead me to the foot of the cross; help me to see Jesus; save my soul this day; end the doubtful strife; answer these questions; bring me, as an humble seeker, to lie before the footstool of thy sovereign mercy, and to receive pardon through the mediatorial sacrifice. "Let him ask—that is all—*let him ask.*"

## IV. Fourthly, the text has in it abundant encouragement for such a seeker.

There are four encouragements here. "Let him ask of

God, *who giveth to all men.*" What a wide statement—Who "giveth to all men!" I will take it in its broadest extent. In natural things, God does give to all men life, health, food, raiment. Who "maketh his sun to rise on the evil and on the good;" who causeth the rain to descend upon the fields of the just and of the unjust. Every creature is favoured with divine benevolence; and there is not a creature, from the tiniest ephemera which creepeth upon the green leaf of the forest, up to the swift-winged angel who adoringly flies upon his Master's will, which is not made to partake of the gifts of the Great Father of Lights. Now, if God hath gifts for all men, how much more will he have gifts for that man who earnestly turns his tearful eye to heaven and cries, "My Father, give me wisdom, that I may be reconciled to thee through the death of thy Son"? Why, the grass, as Herbert says, never asked for the dew, and yet every blade has its own drop; and shall you daily cry for the dew of grace, and there be no drop of heaven's grace for you? Impossible. Fancy your own child saying, "My father, my father, I want to be obedient, I want to be holy;" and suppose that you have power to make your child so, could you find it in your heart to refuse? No; it would be a greater joy to you to give than it could be to the child to accept.

But it has been said, the text ought not to be understood in that broad sense. Very probably it ought not so to be. I conceive that there is implied the limitation that God giveth to all *who seek.* Though the limitation is not stated, yet I think it is intended, because of spiritual mercies God does not give to all men liberally. There are some men who live and die without the liberal favours of grace, because they wantonly and wickedly refuse them; but he gives to all true seekers liberally. We may take that view of it, and we may find you hundreds of witnesses to prove the truth of it, and can find them in this very place this morning. Here is one witness; I myself personally sought the Lord, and he heard me, and delivered me from all my fears. My dear brethren, and my sisters too, I know you could spring up like a great army, if it were a fitting thing to ask you to do, and you could say, " 'This poor man cried, and the Lord heard him.' 'The God of Jacob hath not despised nor abhorred the cries of his people.' " Now, soul, if God has heard so many who sought his face, why should not he hear you? Is it not a comfort to think that hundreds, thousands, and tens of thousands have gone to God, and there never has been a case in which he has refused one? Will he begin with you? Shall you be the first rejected seeker? Oh! then, what a strange destiny yours will be, to have to say in another world, "I am the first who sought grace, and found it not; I wept at the foot of the cross, and I found no mercy; I said, 'Lord, remember me,' but he would not remember me." You will never be able to say that. Hell will never make its boast over such a case; heaven will never have its honour tarnished by one such solitary instance. Seek the Lord and his strength; seek his face evermore. Your hearts shall live that seek him.

The next comfort is, he gives to all men *liberally*. God does not give as we do, a mere trifle to the beggar, but he bestows his wealth by handsful. Solomon asked for wisdom: God gave him wealth and power. In nearly every instance of prayer in the Old Testament, God gives ten times as much as is asked for. Jacob asked that he might have bread to eat, and raiment to put on: God made him to be two bands. The Lord will "do exceeding abundantly above all that we ask or think." This is the divine habit. He not only redeems his promises, but when he might meet them in silver he prefers to pay them in gold. He is exceedingly bountiful. Dear hearers, we have found him so when we have tried him, and do you think he will begin to be niggardly with you? If he should liberally forgive your sins, he will be none the poorer; if he should withhold forgiveness, he will be none the richer. Why should he stint his favour? You want to wash away your sins: there is a river of grace to wash in. You want grace to refresh your souls: he has floods to pour upon the dry ground. We read of the unsearchable riches of Christ. Ho! ye leviathan sinners, here is an ocean of mercy for you to swim in. Ho! you elephantine sinners, here is an ark large enough to hold you and float you above the waters of the deluge! Ho! ye gigantic sinners, whose sins of pride reach up to heaven, and whose feet of lust are plunged in the mire of hell, the sacred hiding-place is large enough to hide even you. The Lord is great in mercy. Oh! who would not ask of so liberal a God, whose thoughts are as high above our thoughts as the heavens are above the earth.

It is added as a third comfort, "*and upbraideth not.*" That is a sweet word. If you help a friend who is in debt, and wants to borrow money, you say, "Remember, I do not like it, you ought not to be in such a state." Your brother wants some aid; you have helped him many times, and will again, but still you upbraid him and tell him he is very imprudent; he ought not to get into these messes; he ought to manage his business better." If you do not tell him so with the mouth, you look at him, and he thinks to himself, "It's very kind of him to give me the help, but really it is very humiliating to me to have to ask of him, because I get so severe a lesson." I suppose we do right to upbraid. I have no doubt we do so with good motives. But God never does upbraid seeking souls. He giveth liberally, and does not dim the lustre of his grace by harsh rebukes. He does not say, "Ah! you sinner, how came you to commit such sin; I will forgive you, but ——." The Father does not talk thus to the returning prodigal. One would have supposed that when the prodigal came back, the father would have said, "Well, dear boy, you are forgiven, but never let me see you do that again. How wrong of you to take that portion of my goods, and spend it in that way! I shall never be so well off as before; you have wasted half my living; and now think where you have been: what a dishonour you have cast upon your father's name and character through wasting your living with harlots. I forgive: I cannot forget." My brethren, it was not so. The prodigal remembered his sins, but his father forgot them all, and exclaimed with joy, "This my son was dead, and is alive again; he was lost, and is found." O soul, if thou didst but know the heart of the Saviour, thou wouldst not tarry in sin. If thou couldst but know the overflowing love of the divine Father, thou wouldst not linger in unbelief."

"His heart is made of tenderness,

His bowels melt with love."

Fool as thou art, be not such a fool as to be unwilling to ask for wisdom, but now breathe the prayer, "Teach me, O God, to trust thy dear Son this day."

Then comes the last encouragement. "*It shall be given him.*" Looking through my text last night, I asked the question—Is that last sentence wanted? "Let him ask of God, which giveth to all men liberally, and upbraideth not." Now, if the Lord gives to all men, he will certainly give to the seeker. Is that last promise wanted? And I came to this conclusion, that it would not have been there if it was not required. There are some sinners who cannot be contented to draw obvious inferences; they must have it in black and white. Such is the fearfulness of their nature, they must have the promise in so many express words. Here they have it, "it shall be given him." You are not left to suppose that it shall be, or to infer that it may be, but it is written, "it shall be given him."

But to whom shall it be given? If *any of you lack wisdom.* "Well," says one, "I am quite out of all catalogues; I am one by myself." Well, but you are surely contained in this "*any of you.*" "Ah!" says one, "but I have a private fault, a sin, an offence which I would not dare to mention, which I believe has damned me for ever." Yet the text says, "If *any of you.*" If I saw a door open, and it said "If *any of you* be hungry, let him come in here," I should not stop outside because I feared that I was not quite the person intended, I should say "It is their business who mean to keep me out, to be more specific in their invitation. They have put it '*any of you*.' I am certainly one of the sons of men, and I will step in to the feast." Ah soul! if God had meant to shut thee out, he would have been more plain about it, but here is not a shutting-out word at all. It says, "If any of you lack wisdom"—well, that is you, surely—that lack of wisdom helps to include you within the boundary. It does not limit the character; it widens it to you, because you feel how foolish you are. The promise is, "it shall be given him." "Suppose I do not get it," you say. You must not suppose God to be a liar. How can you suppose such a blasphemy? "Let him ask of God, and *it shall be given him*." "But," says one, "suppose my sins should prove to be too great!" I cannot, will not suppose anything which can come in conflict with the positive word of God. "Let him ask of God, and it shall be given him." Do you think God does not mean what he says? O sinner, will you add to all your other sins this sin of thinking that God would lie? O man, he invites you to ask of him wisdom, and he says he will give it to you; doubt not the Lord, distrust not the veracity of Jehovah, but come at once humbly, tremblingly, to the foot of the Saviour's cross. View him lifted on high, as the great atoning sacrifice; look to his streaming wounds; behold his brow still covered with the crimson drops which flow from the wounds caused by his thorny crown. Look to him and live. There's life in a look at the Crucified One: look to him, and the promise is that you shall be saved. I commend the text to the careful, thoughtful, believing acceptance of every sinner here. Ask that the sun may not go down until you each and all have received the promise which the text presents to you. May the Holy Spirit now give his own blessing, for Jesus' sake. Amen.

# ABOUT THE AUTHOR

Charles Haddon Spurgeon, known as "The Prince of Preachers", was a famous Reformed Baptist preacher born in Essex, England in 1834. A full-time preacher by the age of 17, Spurgeon preached an estimated 3,600 sermons by the time of his death in 1892. Spurgeon frequently preached to audiences larger than 10,000, while his printed sermons reached tens of thousands more each week.

Spurgeon authored almost 50 volumes including the classic works *All of Grace, Morning & Evening, The Power of Prayer in a Believer's Life, Lectures to My Students,* and *The Treasury of David: A Commentary on the Psalms.* More than a century after his death, Spurgeon's devotional writings continue to touch hearts around the world. Once when asked the secret of his success, Spurgeon replied, "My people pray for me."

# MINISTRIES WE LOVE

Cross-Points Books loves organizations committed to building Christ's church by proclaiming the gospel, resourcing leaders, and training workers for the harvest. Here are some of our favorite ministries:

**9Marks** — Building Healthy Churches (www.9marks.org)

**Desiring God** — Helping people understand and embrace the truth that God is most glorified in us when we are most satisfied in him. (www.desiringgod.org)

**Leadership Resources** — A global ministry training pastors in 30+ countries to preach expository sermons, train other expositors, and foster movements of God's Word. (www.leadershipresources.org)

**Matthias Media** — An evangelical publisher of gospel-centered resources. (www.matthiasmedia.com)

**The Gospel Coalition** — Encouraging and educating Christian leaders by advocating gospel-centered principles and practices that glorify the Savior and do good to those for whom he shed his life's blood. (www.thegospelcoalition.org)

**The Spurgeon Center** — Making visible the life, legacy, and library of Charles Haddon Spurgeon. (center.spurgeon.org)

**Unlocking the Bible** — Delivering the gospel through modern media. The teaching ministry of Colin S. Smith. (www.unlockingthebible.org)

# CONNECT WITH CROSS-POINTS

For news on upcoming releases and deals on resources
promoting sound doctrine and godly devotion,
visit Cross-Points.org or follow us on social media.

Printed in Great Britain
by Amazon